Credits

Editing: Menno van der Veen, Jan Willem Duyvendak
Copy editing: Frances Arnold
Design: Moker Ontwerp, i.s.m. Wonderwerk
Printing: Wilco Art Books
Publisher: Marcel Witvoet, nai010 publishers

This publication is part of the r-link research programme that was funded by the Dutch Scientific Organisation NWO as part of the VerDus SURF programme Smart Urban Regions of the Future.

nai010 publishers is an internationally orientated publisher specialized in developing, producing and distributing books in the fields of architecture, urbanism, art and design. www.nai010.com

nai010 books are available internationally at selected bookstores and from the following distribution partners:

- North, Central and South America - Artbook | D.A.P., New York, USA, dap@dapinc.com
- Rest of the world - Idea Books, Amsterdam, the Netherlands, idea@ideabooks.nl

For general questions, please contact nai010 publishers directly at sales@nai010.com or visit our website www.nai010.com for further information.

ISBN 978-94-6208-631-9
NUR 648
BISAC ARC010000

Participate! (book) also available as e-book:
ISBN 978-94-6208-640-1 (PDF)

PARTICIPATE!

This book should have been written with our beloved colleague, Professor Leonie Janssen-Jansen. But she passed away in 2018 at the age of 42.

For Leonie
(1975-2018)

PAR TICI PATE!

PORTRAITS OF CITIES AND CITIZENS IN ACTION

Edited by Menno van der Veen & Jan Willem Duyvendak

nai010 publishers

Table of content

FOREWORD

Foreword

Martina Löw

More people than ever before want to live in big cities today. With the promise of offering opportunities and prospects for everyone, the modern city remains one of the most worthwhile human ideals, although it has been described as a cold and alien place, not only by Jean-Jacques Rousseau, Karl Marx and Theodor W. Adorno. Even Georg Simmel, in his early sociological writings, deplored the anonymity of the metropolis. Interestingly, however, these implications do not appear to genuinely bother anybody. In this context, it is striking that the question of how and in which way cities use different approaches to urban development to create environments that touch and inspire people and (ideally) stimulate a sense of happiness or contentment, has as yet hardly played a part in urban research.

Who wouldn't know the strange sense of discomfort in a particular city because it somehow doesn't feel right for you? Maybe it's because it seems too typically Catholic, too Protestant (or too Buddhist or Islamic, for that matter)? Perhaps there are too many new buildings and properties, or too many old ones? Or, there is an overall sense of people seeming to be too carefree or too serious? On the other hand, we all are familiar with the opposite experience – an instant sense of being able to breathe freely as you set foot into an unknown city, which makes you feel at ease and in tune with the surroundings. It is hard to be able to determine what makes the difference. What makes cities 'tick' is different in each case. Recent findings suggest that in every city there are specific patterns of interpretation and ways of doing things that evolve, which in turn shape the identity, the state of mind, and the perceptions of the city's inhabitants in different ways.[1] At the

1 S. Frank, P. Gehring, J. Griem and M. Haus, (eds.), *Städte unterscheiden lernen. Zur Analyse interurbaner Kontraste* (Frankfurt am Main/New York: Campus Verlag, 2014)

same time, this intrinsic logic of the city is also regularly reproduced through the dominant local planning practices and routines.

Let's take the city of Darmstadt in Germany as an example: an analysis of seven publicly led rounds of debates asking 'What is typical about Darmstadt?' revealed that the city seems to structurally possess a specific 'emotional' makeup reflected in an all-pervasive effort to create harmony, order and deceleration effects.[2] There is a social climate suggesting that in general the inhabitants are rather content with their city. Predominantly, Darmstadt is experienced as a calm and inherently consistent place, where routinized practices are highly valued as they convey a sense of normalcy and familiarity. If Darmstadt were a person, she'd be probably classified as the phlegmatic type in terms of temperament and character. There is a general sense that this city is able to keep its calm, no matter what happens. By and large, the impression prevails that problems can be solved through conflict prevention; unhurried decision making; communicating with each other to find a compromise; through processes of negotiation; and not least by creating a friendly atmosphere to get to know each other better. This specific 'emotional' culture, it turns out, is typical of Darmstadt. It is recreated structurally and manifestly throughout the city's institutions at different times on various levels by varying groups of people, professionals and individuals. Moreover, this specific culture has a profound effect on the people who live in Darmstadt. Which, of course, is not to imply that all Darmstadters would always go about things in slowed down and relaxed ways in any circumstances. But it means that all inhabitants regularly have to deal (or, at times, struggle) with these intrinsic emotional structural dynamics of the city. For some, Darmstadt's serene nature might be irritating; others might value it highly. In any event, it is the city itself that provides the structuring frame suggestive of specific interpretations and preferred ways of doing and perceiving things.

The book *Participate! Portraits of Cities and Citizens in Action,* edited by Menno van der Veen and Jan Willem Duyvendak, is the first in-depth study to explore the relationship between urban development approaches, intrinsic city logics, and forms of participation in urban contexts. Six dense descriptions and portraits of cities as different as Berlin, Hamburg, Paris, Lyon, Amsterdam and Groningen offer a fresh approach to important questions such as: Where and how do

---

2 M. Löw, P. Noller, S. Süß, (eds.), *Typisch Darmstadt. Eine Stadt beschreibt sich selbst* (Frankfurt am Main/New York: Campus Verlag, 2010)

inhabitants experience problems with their city of residence? What issues are they most affected by? Which action and participation opportunities do they see for themselves in their city?

For the German city of Frankfurt am Main, the philosopher Andreas Großmann showed that arising problems and urban issues are usually taken as a welcome opportunity to underline the city's general ability to (re-)act adequately and efficiently under any circumstances[3]. Traffic problems, for instance, are often interpreted in the affirmative, as a positive display of Frankfurt's image as a busy, dynamic, hard-working place. Frankfurt's local media like to refer to the city as 'the capital' which is able to shape, if not invent, the future proactively and in due course. The German city of Dortmund, on the other hand, seems to focus more on restricting options for acting rather than promoting active citizenship and opportunities for problem-solving. The dominant view is that in the face of difficulties there is nothing to be done. A highly developed sense of constancy, if not immutability, helps to nurture the idea that these difficulties have 'always' been there, and swift action therefore seems as unrealistic as it seems ineffective. At the same time, there is a strong sense of unity articulated not only in Dortmund's soccer stadium but also by a general readiness to agree on and respect common rules and a common fate.

The authors of the volume *Participate!* have discovered similar structural patterns in their studies of Berlin, Hamburg, Paris, Lyon, Amsterdam and Groningen. For the first time, there is ample evidence that participation opportunities and the forms of participation are clearly dependent on the intrinsic logic of a city. As a rule, people identify to a high degree with the city they live in, simply because it is difficult to live in an environment one dislikes. A life in Dortmund is clearly different from a life in Frankfurt. In Dortmund, people are rooted in an environment which strongly emphasizes inclusion in a community, but which is also less conducive to looking optimistically to the future and developing a belief in making change happen.
Frankfurt, on the other hand, seems to instil efficient acting and a self-confident attitude in its inhabitants. Asked how they would describe Frankfurt as a person, residents often describe the city as a 'diva' of sorts: always in the spotlight, shrouded in charisma and a kind of magic. Dortmund, by contrast, is experienced

---

3 A. Großmann, 'Wendungen der Dringlichkeit', in: Frank et al (eds.) *Städte unterscheiden lernen*, op. cit. (note 1), 43-68

as masculine and very 'authentic' – unfussy, without frills and with its heart in the right place.[4] It certainly makes a difference whether you spend your life with a diva or a down-to-earth guy, and many people have a clear preference with regard to these alternatives.

The intrinsic logic of a city does not stop short at architecture and urban planning schemes. On the contrary, cities are regularly developed and re-developed according to their intrinsic logic. A good example is Bremerhaven, a historic seaport in Germany. As Helmuth Berking and Jochen Schwenk (2011) have shown, the city had to learn the hard lesson that the structural transition from seaport to modern service city is difficult to make.

An overwhelming sense of spaciousness but also emptiness dominates the central area of Bremerhaven. Despite the port moving years ago, Bremerhaven's formative period as a seaport during industrial-capitalist times still shows a high degree of continuity. The emptiness triggers an intense awareness of the fact that the city was once built for, and is still focused on, ensuring the swift and smooth distribution of people and goods out into the world. This place clearly won't detain anyone or anything for long. It makes its inhabitants feel that they live in a permanent state of transition and temporariness. A low degree of identification with the city and high migratory flows are the consequences. In new buildings, too, the past is cast in concrete, as they often take the shape of huge ships. Even more striking is how the motifs and images of the past are not only reflected in the city's architecture, but also in urban planning processes, which seem to programmatically hold on to (re-)creating emptiness in the city centre for ever. Visitors to Bremerhaven can't help wondering why so many places in the centre seem so vast, so large and so empty. It fits into the picture that the city has failed to create new content in terms of self-definition and self-identity to this day. Ready at all times to let anyone and anything go out into the world, there is not a single point of attraction in the centre which would signal an initial attempt on the side of the city to retain people and prevent them from crossing the seven seas. These constructional decisions in favour of openness, emptiness and indeterminate structures have a parallel in the perspective and worldview of the locals who live there. In sociological interviews, both urban professionals and inhabitants of Bremerhaven have reported that they see little chance of shaping a common future with the participation of the local population. Instead, hopes for the future are pinned on the in-migration of fresh groups, and not on mobilizing the potential of Bremerhaven's inhabitants.

---

4 H. Berking, S. Frank, J. Marent and R. Richter, 'Städte als Sozialfiguren', in: Frank et al (eds.) *Städte unterscheiden lernen*, op. cit. (note 1), 337-362

As the examples of Darmstadt, Frankfurt, Dortmund and Bremerhaven show, the intrinsic logic of a city is inscribed in everyday practices and actions in unconscious ways, which also applies for Berlin, Hamburg, Paris, Lyon, Amsterdam and Groningen. The logic is manifest in architecture; it finds its expression in urban planning and development approaches; in the worldview and the ways of speaking of the local population; and even in the participation opportunities in a city.
Let's take a final look at Frankfurt am Main and Dortmund. A discourse analysis of crime novels set in Dortmund found that the city's proper name, 'Dortmund,' is mentioned 108 times per one million words; the name 'Frankfurt,', by contrast, appears 285 times per million in novels set in the financial capital. Names create a sense of identity and meaning. Someone or something is called by its proper name. An analysis of media discourses in/on both cities points in the same direction: 'In Dortmund media, the city's name is rarely mentioned . . . in Frankfurt, like in the novels, the name is mentioned . . . very frequently'.[5] A likely interpretation could be: in Frankfurt, naming practices are reflective of the strong and active orientation towards the city as an agent – it is treated as a subject in its own right, rather than merely providing the background of people's living conditions. This is in line with the findings that Frankfurt's city population is frequently referred to as 'citizens' in both the political and media discourse, as well as in official documents.[6] In Dortmund, however, 'citizen' as a form of address is rarely used, and even less frequently are the terms 'urban society' or 'city society.'
The explorations of cities collected in this volume have more surprising results in store, so I hope you enjoy reading these exciting *Portraits of Cities and Citizens in Action*!

---

5 J. Griem and P. Gehring 'Namen nennen', in: Frank et al (eds.) *Städte unterscheiden lernen*, op. cit. (note 1) 314-336

6 M. Barbehön, 'Leitvorstellungen politischer Handlungsträgerschaft', in: Frank et al (eds.) *Städte unterscheiden lernen*, op. cit. (note 1), 207-246

Bibliography

Barbehön, M. , 'Leitvorstellungen politischer Handlungsträgerschaft', in: Frank, Sybille u.a. (Hg.): *Städte unterscheiden lernen. Zur Analyse interurbaner Kontraste*. (Frankfurt am Main/New York: Campus Verlag, 2014), 207-246

Berking, H., Frank, S., Marent, J. and Richter, R., : 'Städte als Sozialfiguren'. In: Frank, Sybille u.a. (Hg.), *Städte unterscheiden lernen. Zur Analyse interurbaner Kontraste* (Frankfurt am Main/ New York: Campus Verlag2014), 337-362

Berking, H. and Schwenk, J., *Hafenstädte. Bremerhaven und Rostock im Wandel* (Frankfurt am Main/New York: Campus Verlag, 2011)

Frank, S., Gehring, P., Griem, J. and Haus, M., (Eds.), *Städte unterscheiden lernen. Zur Analyse interurbaner Kontraste* (Frankfurt am Main/New York: Campus Verlag, 2014) Griem, Julika; Gehring, Petra: 'Namen nennen'. In: Frank, Sybille u.a. (Hg.), *Städte unterscheiden lernen. Zur Analyse interurbaner Kontraste* [Frankfurt am Main/New York: Campus Verlag, 2014], 314-336

Großmann, A.,: 'Wendungen der Dringlichkeit'. In: Frank, Sybille u.a. (Hg.): *Städte unterscheiden lernen. Zur Analyse interurbaner Kontraste* [Frankfurt am Main/New York: Campus Verlag, 2014], 43-68

Löw, M., Noller, P. and Süß, S., (Eds.), *Typisch Darmstadt. Eine Stadt beschreibt sich selbst* (Frankfurt am Main/New York: Campus Verlag 2010)

INTRODUCTION

Introduction

Cities, Cultural Repertoires and Eigenlogik

Menno van der Veen and Jan Willem Duyvendak

A Question of Culture

In 2017 we conducted interviews on urban development in New York. We went to various boroughs of the city and talked to local activists, politicians, civil servants and scientists. No matter where we found ourselves — somebody's favourite Mexican restaurant in the Bronx, a townhouse in Brooklyn, or on the 25th floor of a university building — the interviewees usually started the conversations in the same way. After listening to us explain the project, its background and goals, they would pause, sit back, then look at us pointedly. 'Before you start asking your questions on citizen participation, you have to be aware of one fact: New York is a pro-development city.'

The significance of this 'fact' may be more ambiguous than it first appears. What does pro-development mean? It seems to imply that the city is not only about building, but also — or even principally — about making profits. But perhaps it means more. Perhaps the statement 'New York is a pro-development city' is also referring to the (imagined) history of the city, and to the alleged attitude of its citizens and the people that run its institutions.

In Paris, respondents behaved in the same manner. They would nod supportively throughout our preamble, then pause for a moment in a way that signalled the imminent sharing of something very important indeed. 'Before you start asking your questions about citizen participation, we have to be clear on one thing: are you talking about Paris within the ring-road? Or Paris outside the ring-road? Because that makes a *world* of difference.'

These two anecdotes both make a crucial point: to understand the impact (or potential impact) of citizen participation in urban development projects, one must look beyond their formal rights in planning procedures. As important is to have an idea of the 'culture' of the city that you are studying. However, the culture of a city — or rather, those aspects of city culture that shape how citizen participation works in the context of urban development — are not self-evident. Of course, if you think about metropoles like Paris and New York, it is likely that you have an idea of the cities' culture based on the books, music, art and movies that address those locations. But does this imply that cities have homogeneous cultures? And how do city cultures relate to urban planning and citizen participation? For starters, when it comes to ideas of a city's culture, first associations are likely to be clichés (think, Paris: revolution, good food, elegance, arrogance; New York: business-attitude, freedom). On delving beyond surface level, you are likely to find many counterexamples, as well as all types of subcultures that come with their own typical traits. But even when cities do not have one coherent culture, each of our interlocutors would still claim that urban development in New York differs from urban development in Portland, and that urban development in Paris differs from practices in Lyon.

We therefore went looking for an approach to citizen participation in urban development that could pay attention to cultural aspects while not claiming that city cultures are homogeneous and ahistorical. We found that in the concept of 'intrinsic logic' (Eigenlogik) of Martina Löw.[1] Intrinsic logic starts from the premise that there is something that makes a city tick. This 'something' exists because it is being produced and reproduced by people that explain themselves and others by what is typical of their city. Thus, there is something performative about saying that New York is a pro-development city, or that in Paris the difference between the city within and outside of the ring-road is paramount. It becomes true, because it is stated by people that are involved in the urban development processes.

The concept of Eigenlogik has roots, therefore, in Thomas theorem, and its assertion that what we believe to be true becomes so through our reactions. Frank, Schwenk, Steets and Weidenhaus connect the dots:

---

1 M. Löw and G. Terizakis (eds.), *Städte und ihre Eigenlogik: ein Handbuch für Stadtplanung und Stadtentwicklung* (Campus Verlag, 2011)

'In accordance with Thomas' theorem, according to what people define as real becomes real in its consequences, and with the knowledge that every scientific approach to the world also finds its inescapable starting point in everyday reality, the city must be taken seriously as a sociological subject. . . . If people, according to the argument of the intrinsic logicians, see cities, for example, as differently attractive, tolerant or worth living in, they will act, for instance, on the basis of this knowledge, and their actions have as a consequence that this status manifests itself: By considering certain cities as strongholds of certain scenes or as locations of specific industries, the presence of these scenes or industries is reinforced and solidified.'[2]

A performative understanding of Eigenlogik fits into the cultural turn that occurred in social sciences and humanities over the past decades. In this turn, not only a re-appreciation took place of 'cultural' factors over 'structural' ones, but culture itself became understood as constructed: as the outcome of discursive practices instead of essential characteristics of 'the reality.' Differences among entities (be they countries, cities or neighbourhoods) are not 'given' but reproduced on a daily basis by all actors involved. On the one hand, this shows a certain malleability of what is perceived to be characteristic for the Eigenlogik of these territorialities. On the other hand, it shows continuity and path dependency: actors are limited in the 'cultural repertoires' available to their context.

Sociologists Michèle Lamont and Laurent Thévenot define these repertoires as 'elementary grammars that can be available across situations and that pre-exist individuals, although they are transformed and made salient by individuals.'[3] These narratives explain what cities are about and empirically document the impact of these grammars on the definition of what is considered to be typically for 'us' in this city compared to others.

---

2 S. Frank, J. Schwenk, S. Steets and G. Weidenhaus, 'Der aktuelle Perspektivenstreit in der Stadtsoziologie', *Leviathan (2013)* 41 no. 2, 204 (translated from German). Original text: *'Entsprechend des Thomas-Theorems, nach dem das, was die Menschen als real definieren, in seinen Konsequenzen real wird und mit dem Wissen, dass auch jeder wissenschaftliche Zugriff auf die Welt seinen unhintergehbaren Ausgangspunkt in der Alltagswirklichkeit findet, muss die Stadt als soziologischer Gegenstand ernst genommen werden. (...) Wenn Menschen, so das Argument der Eigenlogiker Innen, Städte beispielsweise als unterschiedlich attraktiv, tolerant oder lebenswert ansehen, werden sie unter anderem auf Basis dieses Wissens handeln, und ihr Handeln hat als Konsequenz, dass sich dieser Status manifestiert: Dadurch, dass einzelne Städte als Hochburgen bestimmter Szenen oder als Standorte bestimmter Industrien gelten, verstärkt und verfestigt sich die Präsenz dieser Szenen oder Industrien.'*

3 M. Lamont and L. Thévenot, *Rethinking comparative cultural sociology: Repertoires of Evaluation in France and the United States* (Cambridge: Cambridge University Press, 2000), 5

More recently, and in a nod to Lamont and Thévenot's 'repertoire' concept, sociologists Christophe Bertossi and Jan Willem Duyvendak coined the phrase 'historical repertoires'[4] to refer to elementary grammars about how the past is framed in present public debates. That is, ways in which history is used to evaluate and justify the present: 'this is the way we do it here, since we have always done it this way.'

This attention to culture and cultural repertoires also came to the fore in the concept 'city habitus' and in some other concepts:

'"cumulative texture" of urban culture by the US sociologist Gerald D. Suttles has to be mentioned here, as well as research on the "cultural imaginary" of the city or on the city as a landscape of knowledge and taste. Harvey Molotch, Richard Freudenburg and Krista Paulsen speak of the "city character", other authors of the "curriculum vitae" or the "biography" of a city."'[5]

Given the productive use of Eigenlogik in research on cities, we prefer this term for now. We therefore ask ourselves: as a specific historical and cultural repertoire, can Eigenlogik explain why urban development strategies and planning rules differ among cities, even within the same national context, as well as those sharing the same international environment of globalization and neo-liberalization?

Intrinsic Logic, Urban Development and Citizens' Participation

"Intrinsic logic captures the hidden structures of cities as locally well-established, by and large tacitly operative processes of sense making along with their physical, material manifestations. In this sense, intrinsic logic also denotes a constellation of

---

4 C. Bertossi, J.W. Duyvendak and N Foner 'Past in the present: migration and the uses of history in the contemporary era'. *Journal of Ethnic and Migration Studies* (2020) 1–17.

5 J. Wietschorke, 'Anthropologie der Stadt: Konzepte und Perspektiven', in: H. Mieg and C. Heyl (eds) Stadt - Ein interdisziplinäres Handbuch (Stuttgart,Weimar: Metzler, 2013, 204 (translated from German). Original text: *'"kumulativen Textur" städtischer Kultur des US-amerikanischen Soziologen Gerald D. Suttles ist hier ebenso zu nennen wie die Forschungen zum „kulturellen Imaginären" der Stadt oder zur Stadt als Wissens- und Geschmackslandschaft. Harvey Molotch, Richard Freudenburg und Krista Paulsen sprechen vom „City Character", andere Autoren vom „Lebenslauf" oder der „Biografie" einer Stadt.'*

interrelated stocks of knowledge and forms of expression by which (people in) cities coalesce into provinces of meaning. Intrinsic logics are constantly being updated in rule-guided, routinized and materially tenable action and, as the case may be, more or less perceptibly changed 'intrinsically' (that is, in keeping with the given city's typical manner). The concept of intrinsic logic brings focus to the insight that each city 'performs' in a certain way, that a particular city has its distinguished pattern of expression in action, and that these specificities are to that extent reconstructable. City limits cannot be thought of as administrative limits but rather as the limits of the city's meaning — boundaries that can be reconstructed through labels but also through shared experience."[6]

The most important element of intrinsic logic for this book is that it puts upfront that the way in which cities operate depends on notions that exist beyond their administrative systems.

That does not mean that administrative systems do not matter. Rather, in order to understand how these systems play out in practice, and what their limits are, you have to take the various processes of self-understanding of a city — its dominant historical-cultural repertoires — into account.

The word 'portraits' in the book's subtitle refers to this idea. By speaking of portraits, we acknowledge that what we say about cities is an interpretation. In fact, it is a construction that the authors base on interviews and written sources about those historical-cultural notions that matter for the self-understanding of the city (as we have found it in the interviews and sources).

Still, intrinsic logic is not the main or only focus of this book. If we adhere to the metaphor of a portrait, it is rather the colouring of the painting. The chapters that follow provide insights in cities by providing specific examples of citizen participation in urban development projects, and a general account of the context wherein these examples exist. The intrinsic logic elements of the chapters therefore provide another type of context: that of the way in which the various actors of the city interpret their own actions and practices of the city.

In New York, we went to some meetings of community boards and other groups involved in (or confronted with) urban development and interviewed a variety of

---

6 M. Löw, *Soziologie der Städte* (Frankfurt am Main: Suhrkamp Verlag, 2013), 900

people who were community organizers, scientists, or professionals in the field of urban planning and real estate development. One of the most noticeable impressions is that there seems to be a development-discourse in New York that is so vivid, that outsiders and visitors almost instantly become participants. The New York development discourse circles around terms like (re-) zoning, social and affordable housing and the question who the community actually is – and for how much its interests should count - that lives in the area that will be redeveloped

When we, for example, were guided through the Melrose neighborhood by Ed Garcìa Conde of Welcome2theBronx[7], we took part in a conversation about who actually had the right to profit from the new housing projects: newcomers from Manhattan, or the various communities that had lived there for more than one generation. This is just one example of the New York development-discourse that includes questions of rights and entitlements that are as complex as the city itself.

There are probably many reasons why these traits are so easy to notice, but one of them might be that the pro-development attitude of New York and its many countercurrents that put emphasis on architectural heritage and community interests is part of the intrinsic logic of a city that has long been able to make people feel that – even if they would not 'make it' – it would have a place for them.

Critics of Cultural Approaches

The cultural approach to cities, and of the concept of a city's intrinsic logic in particular, can be criticized for various reasons. Perhaps the most important refers to the statement that: cities do not have one culture, they are spatial and administrative constructs that, within their borders, house all types of cultural differences. This is especially true for large cities that are culturally diverse like Paris, London and New York. Related, one might also ask that even if it were possible to identify a singular primary culture, then surely that culture is simply the most dominant one? After all, cultural repertoires are historically related to certain districts and elites, and tend to overlook sub-cultures.

We disagree with those who perceive cities primarily in terms of spatial and administrative boundaries. Of course, city cultures are originally tied to territories. Over

7 https://welcome2thebronx.com

time, however, they can travel way beyond their borders. Emigrants may, for example, aim to rebuild a neighbourhood in the image of their 'lost city.' For example, a group of people in the small Dutch town of Purmerend regard themselves as the 'true Jordanese.' This means that they consider themselves the keepers of the culture of a specific neighbourhood in Amsterdam — 'de Jordaan' — even when they have never lived there (but their parents or grandparents did). Similarly, there are residents of Almere who regard themselves as 'more truly from Amsterdam' than newcomers to the city.

There are also those who bring their culture to a city, which may result in districts like Chinatown, Little India or Little Italy. This can also happen on a neighbourhood level due to large concentrations of a specific group of immigrants — 'a Ghanaian neighbourhood', for example. These groups are likely to adapt to typical traits of a city's (or country's) intrinsic logic. And over time, cities themselves also adapt to the presence of these groups. In this sense, the Eigenlogik of cities transforms over time.

The culture of a city, then, is fluid over time, impossible to fully grasp or pinpoint to a specific place. This does not mean, however, that people live this culture as contingent and constructed: for them, the Eigenlogik is real, experienced and produced in daily practices. Even when these practices differ widely among various local communities, the idea of a city culture is recognized and recognizable for all inhabitants. Even when a specific case is atypical and in itself a counterexample of the city culture as it was defined in written sources or interviews, the actors in that case will, in most circumstances, refer to those typical ideas of a city. They will, for example, state that they have managed (or tried) to fight off the dominance of the typical pro-development culture of New York; or they will state that although a neighbourhood is positioned within the ring road of Paris, its residents regard themselves as outsiders and their general attitude towards urban development has to be understood from that perspective.

A second criticism is not focused on the sub-local level; rather, it speculates how ideas on cities' cultures fit into the homogenizing forces of globalization and neo-liberalism.

Since the 1980s, neo-liberalism has undeniably heavily influenced city politics in all Western countries. The answer to this criticism, therefore, should be the following: is the impact of neo-liberal policies the same in all these cities, irrespective of their Eigenlogik, cultural repertories, and of how the past is mobilized in the present? Assessing the impact of neo-liberalism depends on one's own perspective.[8] If one is looking for similarities across countries and across cities, they can easily be found, often justified in a rather similar neo-liberal discourse. However, if one instead looks at the different ways and degrees those neo-liberal projects affect various cities, urban development and citizens' participation, evidence of variety is similarly abundant.

Thereby the big generalizations of neo-liberalism that are said to result in very similar processes of gentrification are replaced by a type of explanation that does not accept *a priori* these generalizations to provide a meaningful framework of analysis. The authors of this book force themselves to put the specificity of a city upfront and only look at the bigger (global economic) context if relevant. Thereby, in the end, the reader gets to know more about the meaning of global tendencies for a specific city. In the chapter of Amsterdam, for example, the authors show how Amsterdam is subject to many policies and trends that can be defined as neo-liberal. At the same time, and as illustrated by specific case studies, its strong tradition of social housing, negotiation and protest, and social policies, also make it resilient to many of neo-liberalism's harshest effects.

So, despite these critical arguments being worthy of examination, the chapters provide sufficient ammunition to look for cities' specificities: for their Eigenlogik.

---

8 B. Waterhout, F. Othengrafen and O. Sykes, 'Neo-liberalization processes and spatial planning in France, Germany, and the Netherlands: An exploration', *Planning Practice & Research* (2013) 28 no.1, 141-159.

Positioning the Book and the City Chapters

Much of the literature on citizen participation is focused on general processes and mechanisms. By adding the concept of intrinsic logic to the portraits of cities, the authors of the various chapters show how participation also works within the specific historical and cultural context of a city.

We present portraits of two cities of the Netherlands, France and Germany. By doing so, readers will get an idea of these cities and how they operate within their national system. They will have an idea of what is typical of the cities, and what are dominant features of the national system. By presenting different cases of urban development within the cities, we acknowledge that also within cities differences may exist.

Some Key Elements of the National Planning Systems of the Netherlands, Germany and France

Because cities exist within their national institutional context, it is useful to describe some of the main traits of the national planning systems in which they operate.

Germany

The German planning system is typically known for its comprehensive approach. After the re-unification of East and West Germany in the 1990s, the West German system was adopted for the whole country. This system differentiates between four levels of planning: federal, state (*Land*), regional and municipality. The system uses the principle of subsidiarity to ensure that planning decisions are being taken on the local level if there is no specific reason to take them on a higher level. Despite this principle of autonomy for municipalities, an important ideal of German planning is to create equal living conditions across the country. This is achieved by evening out large financial differences between regions and states by state investments and redistribution of tax proceeds.

Alongside the comprehensive hierarchical structure of German planning, there are various sectors that determine and finance the development of specific public goods such as housing and infrastructure. As a result, the importance of the planning strategies on the municipal, regional, state and federal level should not be overestimated as many important topics are dealt with (and financed) by these sectors.[9]

In recent years, the German system has given way to a more heterogenous approach to planning. In 2006, the Federal state lost its authority to set frameworks for spatial planning, thereby handing over the authority to make such frameworks to the states (*Länder*). At the same time, the concept of informality has gained importance in the system,[10] meaning that authorities are more open to ad hoc solutions to planning challenges (which may result in temporary uses or mixed uses of specific areas). Finally, Germany is making a transition from an industrialized, fossil fuel-driven economy to a more ecologically sustainable model. This results in the creation of sustainable and green areas, and in the ambition to implement smart models of land use (for example, integrating shopping malls and office centers in one area to prevent sprawl).

The two cities that are discussed in this book, Hamburg and Berlin, are known for their specific practices and histories. Both hold unique positions in the German planning system: While Berlin, the capital of the re-united Germany, stands out for its multi-layered history, Hamburg has become known for its entrepreneurship. Though both cities are city-states,they feature the overall characteristics of the German planning system. These include finding new uses for obsolete industrial buildings, large investments due to the financial redistribution system, and the recent trend of allowing for more types of informality.

The Netherlands

The Dutch planning system is also known for its comprehensive approach. Indeed, it was once characterized as a 'planner's dream' due to its integral approach to city planning, which meant that planning of neighbourhoods was based on a cooperative effort of municipalities, housing corporations, architects and other stakeholders. On paper, the Dutch system looks very similar to the German: there is a national level, provincial, regional and municipal levels. However, after 2001

---

9 H. Blotevogel, R. Danielzyk, and A. Münter 'Spatial planning in Germany' in M. Reimer, P. Getimis, and H. Blotevogel (eds) *Spatial Planning Systems and Practices in Europe*, (New York: Routledge, 2014), 83-108

10 Blotevogel et al., *Spatial Planning*, op. cit. (note 11)

when the fifth National Planning Brief was published, the Dutch government did away with a comprehensive national approach to planning. Meanwhile, it is in the process of implementing a national environmental act that sets out the standard procedures for all planning initiatives.

As with the German system, the principle of subsidiarity results in municipalities being key players in planning. This autonomy principle has for a long period been enforced by municipalities' – relatively – well-funded position. Cities therefore were able to use active strategies to acquire land for the realization of commercial districts and finance public facilities with the proceeds. However, during the last 15 years this situation has changed and municipalities have been looking at various models to cooperate with market parties. They are thereby retaining an active approach to planning, despite no longer being able to finance planning ambitions independently.

In another similarity between systems in the Netherlands and in Germany, many Dutch planning projects are financed by specific (national) funds. The most important of these funds are those for (social) housing, infrastructure projects, and improvement of public transport hubs. Thus, many planning projects in Dutch cities are based on the active role of the municipal government, funding from specific national funds, regional and provincial involvement focussed on the comprehensiveness of the planning proposals and ecological sustainability.

Challenges of the Dutch planning system are the shortage of affordable housing, sustainability, and – as cities continue to grow – dealing with bottom-up initiatives. One could say that Dutch planning is simultaneously confronted with the need for large housing projects on the one hand, and the aim of providing more space for bottom-up initiatives on the other. At the same time, the transition towards sustainable energy results in many land use conflicts. Therefore, it is not unlikely that the Dutch government will implement a new national planning strategy for the upcoming period.[11]

The city chapters Groningen and Amsterdam are illustrative of the active involvement of municipal governments as they present a range of actors and roles within the planning process, including landowner, planning authority and subsidizer.

---

11 B. Needham, *Dutch land-use planning: The principles and the practice* (Farnham: Ashgate, 2014)

The cities are also home to tensions between the aim of providing more room for bottom-up, and informal initiatives, and implementing comprehensive planning schemes on a city or regional scale.

France

The frameworks of urban planning in France are traditionally dealt with on the national level. Based on principles of redistribution of wealth and solidarity, the French national government used to issue nationwide policies for city and regional planning. More recently, this system has shifted its focus more to the municipalities, departments and regions. The national funding for urban development strategies is based on territorial contracts. Instead of dictating planning strategies, the state seeks to partner more with local regions; fund projects and strategies that combine housing, transport and economic initiatives; and promote a degree of competitiveness between regions.[12] At the same time, the traditional focus on rules and planning norms in France is shifting more to a focus on planning projects, thereby promoting integral approaches to planning challenges.

Still, French planning is very much dependent on the activity of public actors, political choices and public investments. During our fieldwork, we were impressed with the various experiments in participation that seem to be tested as part of the initiatives of the *Politique de la Ville*. The system is clearly looking for ways to become more project- and problem-oriented, and less focused on rules and the procedures of political decision making. A recent experiment was a citizen council on climate change — *Convention Citoyen pour le Climate,* which began in 2019 — that periodically invites the participation of 150 randomly chosen citizens.

The city chapters of Lyon and Paris both offer examples of this tradition of government involvement and planning, as well as the shift towards more project- and problem-oriented types of planning, such as participatory budgeting in Paris.

Findings of city chapters

What do the various city chapters tell us about participation? The chapters highlight characteristics of city planning and local culture. Given the results of the case studies presented, we are convinced that local culture greatly shapes the context of participation, and this impact does not seem to be diminishing. The entrepeneurial context of the urban development in Lyon, differs from the elitist

---

12 Waterhout et al., 'Neo-liberalization processes', op. cit. (note 10)

traditions in Paris. The business and freedom culture of Hamburg (the 'Bürger and Outlaw-logic 'as it is referred to in the chapter), results in other planning practices than the 'ever-to-become' tradition of Berlin.

Of course, also the enthusiasm and skills of specific people (such as the entrepreneur behind Toentje urban farm in Groningen, for example) or groups (like the collective in Mitte Altona, Hamburg who fought to maintain the character of their beloved district) greatly impacts outcomes. However, whether inhabitants can be successful participants in urban projects depends on the response of power holders and the way the latter perceive the Eigenlogik of their cities.

In the international literature there is quite some scepticism regarding the 'participation speak' that we came across in all cities covered in this book. Participation is sometimes said to be praised by those who are opposed to real democratic influence of citizens. The decision that a city wants to organize the Olympic Games is taken by a small elite, who – after the decision is taken – uses participation speak to ensure that all types of new projects – such as the lay-out of a new Olympic park - will get their shape in a participatory process.
In an important publication *"Democratizing Inequalities: dilemmas of the new public participation"*, Lee et al.[13] raise the pertinent question how the context of increased inequality affects the new forms of participation.
We agree that the context of participation should be taken into account, but disagree that the socioeconomic context is then the only one, or even the most relevant one. Sure, as the upcoming chapters will show, in many cities inhabitants with entrepreneurial skills are privileged in the new forms of participation.[14] However, even in similar contexts of increasing inequalities, some cities are better able to also reach out to less privileged citizens. They feel this is their duty, given their culture, history and Eigenlogik.

Since in many cities in the past decade the context of city building has become more conflictual, the 'usual way' to do things is under pressure. However, it is precisely under these homogenizing circumstances of city building that the hypothesis of the pertinence of Eigenlogik can be tested.

---

13 C.W. Lee, M. McQuarrie, and E.T. Walker, *Democratizing Inequalities: Dilemmas of the New Public Participation*. (New York: NYU Press, 2015)
14 E.W. Stapper and J.W Duyvendak, 'Good residents, bad residents: How participatory processes in urban redevelopment privilege entrepreneurial citizens', *Cities* (2020), 107

Bibliography

Bertossi, C., Duyvendak, J.W. and Foner, N., 'Past in the present: migration and the uses of history in the contemporary era'. *Journal of Ethnic and Migration Studies* (2020) 1–17.

Blotevogel, H. Danielzyk, R. and Münter, A. 'Spatial planning in Germany' in *Reimer, M. Getimis, P. and Blotevogel, H. (eds) Spatial Planning Systems and Practices in Europe*, (New York: Routledge, 2014), 83-108

Frank, S., Schwenk, J., Steets, S., & Weidenhaus, G. Der aktuelle Perspektivenstreit in der Stadtsoziologie. *Leviathan* (2013), 41(2), 197–223.

Lamont, M., & Thévenot, L. Rethinking comparative cultural sociology: *Repertoires of Evaluation* in France and the United States (Cambridge: Cambridge University Press, 2000)

Lee, C. W., McQuarrie, M., & Walker, E. T. (Eds.) *Democratizing Inequalities: Dilemmas of the New Public Participation*. (New York: NYU Press, 2015)

Löw, M., *Soziologie der Städte* (Frankfurt am Main: Suhrkamp Verlag, 2013)

Löw, M. and Terizakis, G. (Eds.), *Städte und ihre Eigenlogik: ein Handbuch für Stadtplanung und Stadtentwicklung* (Campus Verlag, 2011)

Molotch, H., Freudenburg, W., & Paulsen, K. E. History repeats itself, but how? City character, urban tradition, and the accomplishment of place. *American Sociological Review* (2000), 791-823.

Needham, B., *Dutch land-use planning: The principles and the practice* (Farnham: Ashgate, 2014)

Stapper, E. W., & Duyvendak, J. W., 'Good residents, bad residents: How participatory processes in urban redevelopment privilege entrepreneurial citizens', *Cities* (2020), 107, 102898

Waterhout, B., Othengrafen, F., & Sykes, O., 'Neo-liberalization processes and spatial planning in France, Germany, and the Netherlands: An exploration', *Planning Practice & Research* (2013) 28 no.1, 141-159.

Wietschorke, J., 'Anthropologie der Stadt: Konzepte und Perspektiven', in: H. Mieg and C. Heyl (eds) *Stadt - Ein interdisziplinäres Handbuch* (Stuttgart,Weimar: Metzler, 2013)

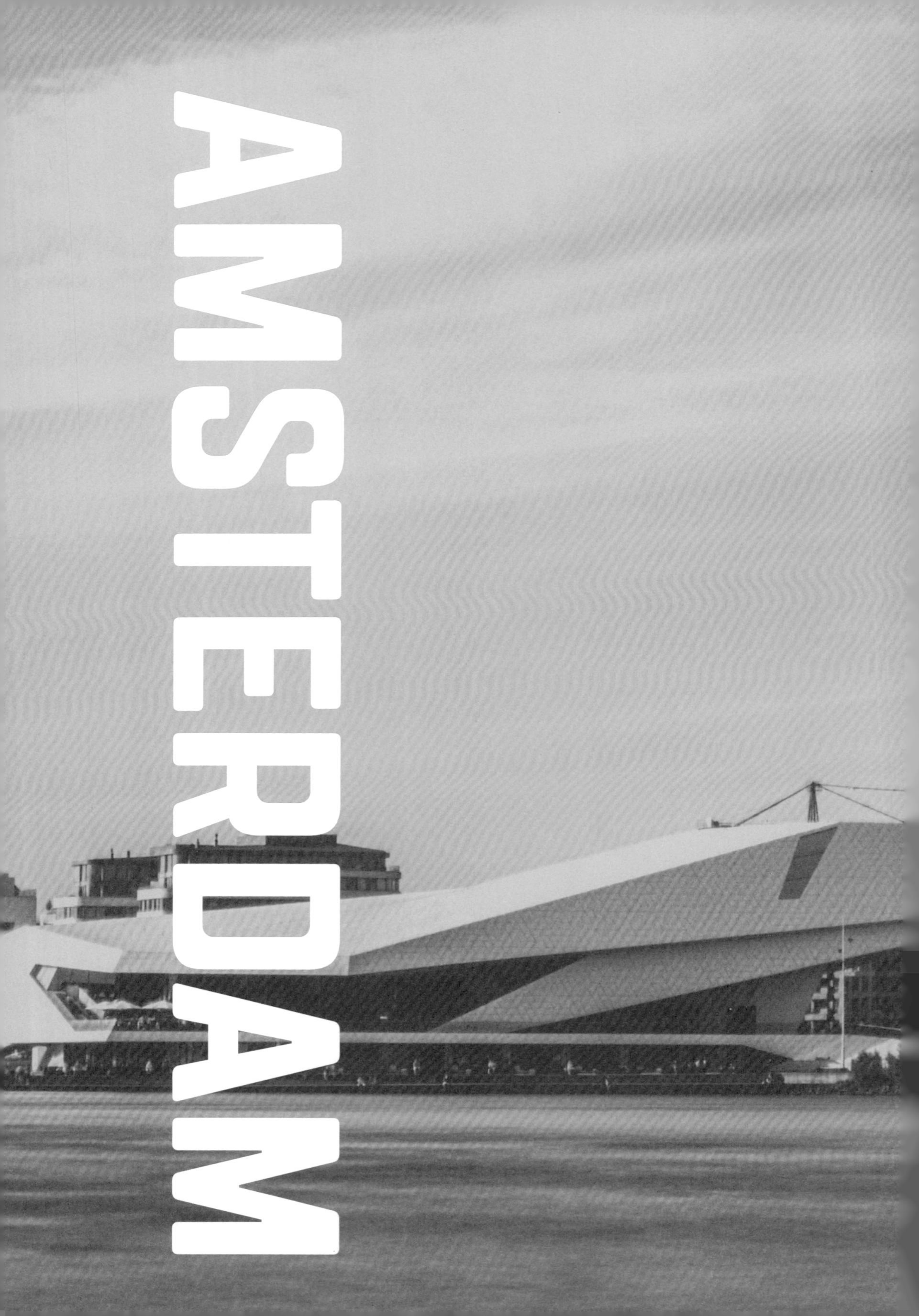
AMSTERDAM

LOOKOUT

A City of Strong Government and Active Citizens

Eigenlogik Amsterdam

Karin Christof and Stan Majoor

The Dutch capital of Amsterdam has a proud tradition of government-steered urban interventions over the last century. However, at the same time, the city can be characterized by a strong civil society taking an active interest in its development. Following a shift towards neoliberal policies in the last few decades, Amsterdam has struggled to change its course of top-down steered urban planning. As illustrated in this chapter through two of Amsterdam's recent development projects, the city has steered towards more market-oriented approaches *and* citizen participation. It is in this continuous confrontation between a strong government and outspoken civil society that the city's possible Eigenlogik of pragmatic cooperation becomes visible.

Most histories of the Netherlands start with its enduring fight against the forces of water. Amsterdam is no exception, and has had to defend itself when houses sank into its muddy soil. The city only came to life properly around 1250 when it built a dam over the Amstel: a drainage canal for the peat bogs with a sluice to discharge into the River IJ. It is from this Middle Ages intervention that Amsterdam gets its name. Today, Amsterdam is part of a conglomerate of cities in the heavily urbanized Rhine-Meuse-Scheldt delta. The region around the city is characterized by a polder landscape protected by dikes that require continuous technical support. This high-maintenance landscape below sea-level has long demanded active cooperation between government, institutions and residents, evidenced in historic (and ongoing) systematic interventions such as land consolidation and reclamation projects.[1] The cooperative attitude to safeguarding collective and individual goals has come to be regarded as a characteristic of the Dutch society and planning tradition. Working against the forces of water has contributed to a culture that, due to pragmatic necessity, is focused on cooperation.[2] It is no coincidence, then, that the term *polderen* has been used in Dutch politics to designate the process of finding a compromise that suits as many stakeholders as possible. Alluding to the country's consensus-based policymaking, it has increasingly extended to finding solutions for social problems not only between political parties but also between government and civil society. This development has been fast-tracked by an economizing Dutch social welfare state.

Before analysing two contemporary cases as present forms of this 'urban poldermodel,' we will briefly revisit the main themes in the city's urban development in the last century.

Big Plans Overturned

Amsterdam's contemporary urban planning tradition is backdropped by a powerful government. In the twentieth century, the city's building policies earned international acclaim. This started with 'Plan Zuid' (1904, 1915) and the CIAM-inspired 'General Extension Plan' (1935) that laid the foundation for a major urban extension in the western and southern parts of the city.[3] The strong technocratic basis that underlined the city's major expansions can be explained by the fact that after the Second World War, Dutch politics entered a timeframe with an increasing belief that society was malleable. Government thought that they had the responsibility to 'reconstruct' Dutch society. This belief was based on the premise that people and places could be modelled with the government as the active lead. This idea was visible in both the planning process — without much citizen participation — as well as in the overly planned design of the city's major urban extensions.

---

1 In the Netherlands, water engineering projects have long been managed by local water boards. Founded as public bodies, they were the first local democratic planning institutions that served as independent governance structures to protect communities and safeguard agricultural activities.

2 This pragmatism is also founded in trading: during the so-called Golden Age of the seventeenth century when the then Dutch Republic was a trade empire with worldwide colonies, cooperation was in merchants' interests to negotiate and avoid conflicts or war.

3 The extensions in Amsterdam South-East (the Bijlmer) and North that were developed from the 1960s onwards can be seen as structural additions to this General Extension Plan.

Beginning in the mid- to late-twentieth century, Amsterdam's urban planning gradually started to integrate more democratic and decision-making tools for direct citizen involvement. This shift was in response to criticism of the heavily top-down approach to development projects that had gone before; a planned city-making that was strongly contested on an international scale. The profound critique surrounding the top-down urban approach led to seminal debates on urban development, spearheaded internationally by the likes of Jane Jacobs and Henri Lefebvre. In the regeneration of inner-city neighbourhoods, citizens asked for strategies that built from residents' perspective — rather than the experts working for governmental organizations. Activists, tenants and squatters protested heavily in the 1970s and 1980s in Amsterdam, as in other European cities, against the demolition of whole neighbourhoods and real estate speculation. The Nieuwmarkt riots in 1975 were a culmination point in the Dutch capital. The civic claims were directed towards the demolition of housing to make way for a highway and metro line through inner-city districts and asked for the renovation of the buildings, and a subsequent guarantee of affordable social rents.

Citizens opposed the oftentimes technocratic tabula rasa projects which were heavily influenced by modernistic urban planning beliefs to 'upgrade' the inner city and abutting neighbourhoods. These included the realization of high-rise housing and an emphasis on car transport. After much protest, the winds of change started to be felt in Amsterdam. This shift is visible in the structure plans that the city made for its long-term spatial investments. While the plans of the 1950s and 1960s were still insisting on a thorough 'modernization' of the historic core, including large demolitions and new infrastructures, the plans of the 1970s and onwards emphasized a strategy of more careful urban reconstruction. That meant following existing street patterns, and a focus on public participation and affordable housing in inner city renovation projects.[4] This dramatic shift from what turned out to be the final throes of Modernist urban planning to consultation-led participatory processes won international plaudits: Amsterdam was hailed as a just city,[5] and praised for its social democratic principles of city (re-) development.

---

4 A. Jolles, E. Klusman and B. Teunissen, *Stadsplan Amsterdam. Toekomstvisies op de ruimtelijke ontwikkeling van de stad* (Rotterdam: NAi, 2003)
5 S. Fainstein, *The Just City* (Ithaca and London: Cornell University Press, 2010)

Creatives Under Pressure in a Globalizing City

Fast-forward to today and some scholars and residents claim that Amsterdam no longer deserves this 'just city' status.[6] In the last decades, under the same pragmatic culture of economic gain, the city has pursued a dual pathway of development. On the one hand is an emphasis on strong social urban regeneration policies, and on the other, a growing emphasis on urban policies to attract international business, trade and tourism. To that end, the historic inner city has been slowly transformed into a more consumerist space, following the logic of the financial market to satisfy the needs of a booming tourism industry. Along the primary ring road, new office districts like Sloterdijk, Riekerpolder, Zuidas and Bijlmer/Arena have been realized; and expensive owner-occupied housing developments have come to dominate residential plans.[7] With major national investments, Schiphol international airport has been expanded and connected to a new high-speed rail to Belgium and France. This evolution has changed the economy of the city, created many new jobs but also made the city a much more expensive place to live, as witnessed by housing prices of owner-occupied dwellings rising around 10 per cent per annum in recent years.[8]

The reasons behind this decrease in affordable housing are manifold. First, national and European policies have served to weaken the position of housing corporations that still own a major stock of the city's residential properties. In the Netherlands, it was the Heerma Memorandum of 1989 that initiated the privatization of housing corporations.[9] The change in housing policy was a response to the Maastricht Treaty on the European Union that asked member states to keep their public finances within healthy margins, with a member's deficit not surpassing 3 per cent of its GDP. In the 2000s the position of housing corporations was further weakened due to EU regulations postulating that they had to concentrate

---

6 J. Uitermark, 'An in memoriam for the just city of Amsterdam', *City* (2009) 13(2–3), 347–361; P. Marcuse, J. Connolly, J. Novy, I. Olivo, C. Potter and J. Steil (eds.), *Searching for the Just City: Debates in Urban Theory and Practice* (Abingdon and New York: Routledge: 2009)

7 F. Savini, W.R. Boterman, W.P.C. Van Gent and S.J.H. Majoor, 'Amsterdam in the 21st century: Geography, housing, spatial development and politics', *Cities* (2016) 52, 103–113.

8 See CBS, *Bestaande koopwoningen; verkoopprijzen; regio; prijsindex 2015=100* (Den Haag: Centraal Bureau voor de Statistiek, Statline, 2021). https://www.cbs.nl/nl-nl/cijfers/detail/83913NED

9 Heerma, E. (1989), Volkshuisvesting in de jaren negentig (Housing in the nineties), Second Chamber 1988-1989, 20.691 Nos. 2-3, The Hague: SDU, 27 April.

their (subsidized) activities exclusively on low-income families. This was a break in tradition from their original lower *and* middle-class orientation. At the same time, city campaigns promoting Amsterdam as a hub for the creative, IT, finance and tourist economies stimulated an increase of urban foreign investment in real estate property. Strong planning policies to keep the city compact, in combination with building restrictions due to the vicinity of the airport and seaport, weakened the city's options to create new housing areas within its perimeters.

Beginning in the early 2000s, the impact of this turn towards international competitiveness and an increased pressure on urban space was particularly noticeable in the cultural sector, the importance of which was now heightened both for the city's economy and image. With affordable locations harder to find, the underused post-industrial shores of the River IJ had become a favourite location for squatters, artists and other creatives. When those plots of land came increasingly under pressure from market-oriented redevelopment policies, the last squats at the IJ had to go. In their place came substantial real estate developments that transformed Amsterdam's former industrial waterfront into a metropolitan residential and creative working place, moving the city centre further towards its original seventeenth century harbour site. Before the city embarked on these large-scale urban development projects, the government had to deal with the remaining cultural squats in dilapidated building complexes along the run-down harbour site, such as Vrieshuis Amerika or the Graansilo.

Pragmatic Cooperation with Creatives and Citizens

Although some squats underwent a process of legalization, others had to go. For those forced to close, the city government discussed strategies with a group of former squatters. The goal of this assembly was to prevent the displacement of artists out of the city, and postulated to include subculture as a thriving force for the culture of Amsterdam. Its slogan, 'no culture without subculture,' formed the basis for a Creative Incubator Policy (*Broedplaatsenbeleid)* that was implemented in 2000 with a budget of 45 million Euros. Taking the practice of self-organization to heart, the city of Amsterdam put cultural creativity at the core of its economic activities. Inspired by Richard Florida's extolling of creatives' impact on a city's economy,[10] the policy aimed at incorporating various initiatives and buildings into the city's urban fabric. By offering affordable workplaces, they wanted to maintain the city's status as a creative breeding ground; and provide temporary and

10 R. Florida, *The Rise of the Creative Class* (New York: Basic Books, 2003).

long-term work, plus living spaces for artists and creatives that were protected from the market.[11]

In the period that followed, more than sixty 'breeding places' were redeveloped by 2015 within the Creative Incubator Policy in Amsterdam, including several former squats that were legalized. A municipal office, called the Bureau Broedplaatsen, was put in place to assist anyone interested — from private parties, housing corporations to squatting collectives — in converting buildings into temporary creative incubator places. For the re-use of dilapidated or vacant housing stock, they offered guidance and financial support, and facilitated leasehold agreements with the different stakeholders. The resulting (sub)cultural organizations and collectives of the early 2000s include the NDSM Wharf, Plantage Doklaan, the old Film Academy OT301 and Pakhuis de Zwijger.[12] The latter — a refurbished refrigerated warehouse on the shores of the IJ — was opened as one of the first showcase examples in 2006 to host and exhibit the creative potential of the city of Amsterdam. The Creative Incubator Policy is thereby a prime example of a typical cultural 'polder model' in the city's politics, in so much as it sees a strong city government cooperate with other stakeholders and is open to incorporate additional ideas and concepts. This pragmatic cooperation has created some form of relief for the city's cultural sector in a global city that has fast become much more expensive. In the meantime, the link with counterculture has become increasingly merged into creative policies, with fewer and fewer spaces for cultural activities operating outside of the commercial mainstream.[13]

The complex cooperation between a strong government and a vocal and occasionally powerful citizenry is not only a defining mechanism in the city's policies regarding subcultures and creative industries. As in other Western contexts, recent decades have seen the Amsterdam government's increased dependency upon self-reliant and responsible citizens. This is due to government's gradual withdrawal from public services for reasons spanning social, ideological and

---

11 In the first decade of the 21st century, other cities in the Netherlands followed Amsterdam's example by formulating their own cultural incubator policies, such as The Hague, Rotterdam, and Nijmegen.

12 B. van der Geyn and J. Draaisma, 'The embrace of Amsterdam's creative breeding ground', in: L. Porter and K. Shaw (eds.), *Whose Urban Renaissance? An international comparison of urban regeneration strategies* (London and New York: Routledge, 2009) 202-211

13 While the working and living places within the Creative Incubator Policy were supposed to give space to subculture, they have rather turned into 'economic tools' for creative city branding over time.

financial. As a result, citizen participation in its broadest sense has emerged as a 'missing link' to tackle everything from community development and urban regeneration, to healthcare. This gradual shift was crystallized in a speech to parliament by King of the Netherlands Willem-Alexander in 2013, when he announced that the Dutch welfare state would effectively sidestep to become an active civil society, or 'participatory society.'[14] Next to big cuts in welfare services, citizens have been asked to take more responsibility for their own well-being and that of others to increase value to society at large. This attitude asks for citizens' readiness to not only self-organize their lives but to also provide for weaker members of society such as the elderly or sick. However, this level of decentralization and belief in the active self-reliant citizen has led to public concerns that certain groups tend to be excluded from — or are incapable of — this ideal of active self-reliance.[15] Invariably, a 'participatory society' equates to only those citizens who know whom to address for possible help or funding, have a solid (professional) network, and can volunteer their time. But how does the hype surrounding the Netherlands' shift from one of the world's most comprehensive welfare states to a participation-based one square with the reality of strong government intervention in urban planning?

Engagement Managed in Two Recent Cases?

After the slowdown of the city's development due to the global financial crisis of 2008 to 2009 that affected the city's housing production for several years, Amsterdam started to implement ambitious quantitative targets for large-scale new housing production.[16] These goals exerted severe densification pressure on existing neighbourhoods. Among them are Buiksloterham in Amsterdam-North, a

14 Ministerie van Algemene Zaken, Troonrede 2013. Online. Available HTTP: (Accessed: 20 Feb 2021).

15 F. Bredewold, J.W. Duyvendak, T. Kampen, E. Tonkens, and L. Verplanke, *De verhuizing van de verzorgingsstaat: Hoe de overheid nabij komt* (Amsterdam: Van Gennep, 2018); M. van Twist, N. Chin-A-Fat, J. Scherpenisse and M. van Steen (eds.) *'Ja, maar...': Reflecties op de participatiesamenleving* (Den Haag: Boom Lemma, 2014)

16 T. Koolmees and S.J.H. Majoor. 'Local government in the face of crisis: Changing public management of urban projects in Amsterdam', in: M. Raco and F. Savini (eds.), *Planning and Knowledge: How new forms of technocracy are shaping contemporary cities* (Bristol: Policy Press, 2019). 59-73

mixed-use former harbour area; and K-Neighbourhood in Amsterdam-Southeast. The latter dates from the 1970s, and is part of the Bijlmermeer, the Modernist addition to Amsterdam's General Extension Plan. Both are government initiated and intended as inclusive developments. Where K-Neighbourhood became mired by a forceful government's failure to include the input of participating residents in the first place, Buiksloterham has become a model for incremental development of circular residential and office areas. The latter was set up by private and civic interest groups and ultimately saw the municipality face criticism for backsliding on a position of environmental guardianship in light of an improved economy. Both K-Neighbourhood and Buiksloterham exemplify Amsterdam's urban programme for the coming decades. In the context of growing pressure on the city's land and concerns around social and environmental issues, its direction is focused on brownfield regeneration in the harbour area and densification of the Modernist post-war extensions into more mixed-use neighbourhoods. The cases illustrate how pragmatic cooperation between a strong government and active citizenry could develop the city in a more democratic and environmentally sensitive direction for the future.

Buiksloterham: A Level Playing Field for Civic Stakeholders

Buiksloterham is a brownfield development of a former industrial estate in Amsterdam North, on the Northern shores of the IJ River. When the 100 hectares of land became available for urban development in 1997, the municipality entered negotiations with polluting industrial firms already present in the area. As the municipality could not buy out all businesses, they were forced to approach the development incrementally. That included a flexible approach to zoning as the project developed. A first step was to determine the policy ambitions of the site and use those to help attract investors. In 2011, a legally binding land-use plan came into place that sketched the future development of Buiksloterham — without detailed functions and locations of buildings. This effectively created adjustable zones. That meant the residential focus of a mixed-use zone could be amplified when a company moved from the area, or changed to other production methods with less environmental impact. That businesses have not opposed the development plans can be attributed to early negotiations with the municipality, and the guarantee that their operations would not be hindered after housing has been realized. In addition, investors were sought to incentivize current land users to lessen their environmental impact. This has allowed urban planners to focus on issues of sustainability and self-built housing within an open-ended and so-called 'organic' planning process.[17] To that end, construction of a mixed-use urban zone began in 2005 to be completed by 2030. The figure of the planned 8,600 new houses has doubled within the last decade due to the high pressure on Amsterdam's housing market.[18] Through tenders for innovative sustainable developments, innovative citizen initiatives became engaged. As a result, it soon turned into one of the biggest self-build locations in Amsterdam.

As it turned out, the municipality's step-by-step approach was prescient: the financial crisis of 2008 put a halt to lots of large-scale developments. This turned attention towards Buiksloterham with its small-scale sustainability projects. In order to solve the ecological issues of the highly polluted area and find innovative uses for the site, the city government worked with an active land policy employing tender procedures and concept-based allocations. The first to be realized was De Ceuvel in 2012, which was granted a 10-year ground lease on a former shipyard from the municipality. Sustained by the Creative Incubator Policy for cultural places, De Ceuvel opened in 2014. As a self-governed community for creative and social enterprises, it comprised workspaces in recycled houseboats, a café, event space and guest accommodation. Working with the organization Metabolic whose activities centre on circular economy and how it can be applied to the built environment, De Ceuvel also incorporated off-grid, self-sufficient technologies. Among them were sustainable systems for grey water and heat exchange. Through the different communities and stakeholders involved, circularity became central to the wider urban regeneration project for all participating parties. This includes the 'living lab' Stadslab Buiksloterham, where residents and entrepreneurs explore circular ways of living and working through experiments and research in sustainability. Focus areas span the re-use and recycling of materials, renewable energy, strengthening biodiversity, integrating culture and creating social value that goes beyond financial profits alone.[19] In 2015, adherence to these principles was seemingly made official when the municipality, residents and businesses signed the Manifesto Circular Buiksloterham to ensure these circular

---

17 Municipality of Amsterdam (2009a) Bestemmingsplan "Buiksloterham" [Land use Plan Buiksloterham]. The Netherlands: Municipality of Amsterdam.

18 Van Zoelen, B., 'Is Buiksloterham straks echt zo groen en circulair?' *Het Parool* (6 January 2020) Online. Available HTTP: https://www.parool.nl/nieuws/is-buiksloterham-straks-echt-zo-groen-en-circulair~bc02943f/

19 Metabolic, Studioninedots, and DELVA Landscape Architects, *Circular Buiksloterham: Transitioning Amsterdam to a Circular City: Vision & Ambition* (Amsterdam: Circular Buiksloterham, 2015)

ambitions be realized.[20] Other sustainable buildings and initiatives emerged, such as Patch 22, an energy-neutral wooden housing structure; Schoon Schip, a sustainable floating residential area; and innovative housing development, Cityplot Buiksloterham.[21]

Buiksloterham has been recognized internationally for its smart urban solutions, by the city government of Amsterdam, as well as by creatives and professionals. The outcome of the municipality's call for circular experiments such as the self-organized sustainable communities and housing developments have allowed for different uses, publics and innovation, as evidenced (in theory, at least) by Buiksloterham's circular manifesto. The manifesto, however, transpired to be not so much a binding agreement between stakeholders, but rather a letter of intent. According to entrepreneurs in the area, this change of contractual force was mainly caused by the position of the city of Amsterdam. With ownership of 30 percent of the land,[22] the city of Amsterdam faced challenges in imposing the circular criteria on all private parties and at the same time, realizing much-needed housing in the urban renewal area. Ultimately, it did not want to alter policy agreements, nor face difficult discussions with stakeholders that had already acquired plots of land in Buiksloterham. As landowner, however, only it was positioned to negotiate circular ambitions at a project level.

Residents and entrepreneurs in the area who contributed to developing the area of Buiksloterham have voiced their disappointment as to the actual degree of participation granted by the urban planning department. Their criticism comes down what many see as duplicity on the part of the municipality. Within the tender phase, innovative circular building principles were facilitated by the city government as part of an urban experiment in which it positioned itself as a guardian of the environment. But when the economy picked up again in 2014, the municipality of Amsterdam reverted once again to a financially geared top-down approach and 'traditional' building rules and regulations where building projects were realized outside of tender procedures. Such financial accounting does not allow innovative project development with the use of circular materials.[23]

---

20 Metabolic *et al.*, 'Manifest Circular Buiksloterham', op. cit. (note 19)
21 https://buiksloterham.nl/projecten
22 Gemeente Amsterdam, *Concept Nota van Beantwoording: Behorende bij investeringsnota Buiksloterham 2020*, P. 99
23 B. Hulsman, 'Duurzaam bouwen? Dat wordt lastig met zulke grondprijzen' (18 March 2021) *NRC*. Online. Available HTTP: https://www.nrc.nl/nieuws/2021/03/18/duurzaam-bouwen-dat-wordt-lastig-met-zulke-grondprijzen-a4036011

Instead it asks for a higher commitment and investment that only pays back in a longer time frame. So far, the circular ambitions realized within the innovative community development have therefore remained separate and dispersed sustainable initiatives.

The episode is illustrative of how Amsterdam's international reputation for innovative and sustainable urban development clashes with current pressures on the housing market, rising prices in the city, and the commercial spirit of the city government. Residents who were involved in setting up Buiksloterham from the grassroots during the crisis hoped to contribute to a change in institutional ways of thinking. However, besides model projects within the tender phase, the city's planning department was not able to impose an all-encompassing standard for an integral circular and sustainable neighbourhood development yet. On top of that, citizens involved in the participatory projects from the very beginning voiced their discomfort that they were not approached as experts to discuss urban planning issues in the first instance, but rather as residents who presumably were involved out of self-interest. Through participative formats such as public consultation, the urban pioneers that had been attracted to the innovative area in the first place increasingly voiced their disappointment at sustainable ambitions being green-washed.

K-Neighbourhood: Technocratic Versus Citizen Power

The K-Neighbourhood (*K-buurt*) is located in the Bijlmermeer area, a polder reclamation landscape in Amsterdam's southeast. Set up in the late 1960s as a government-steered Modernistic housing area with high-rise slabs in a green parkland environment, it faced many social and economic challenges. Though the area was designed as a neighbourhood for Dutch middle class families,[24] the affluent, white-collar groups the Bijlmer's architects had originally envisaged instead favoured single-family houses in newly built towns near Amsterdam such as Almere and Lelystad. Incorporating affordable, semi-detached family housing, these new towns were built in the 1970s as land reclamation projects to ease the pressure of the housing market in Amsterdam. Therefore, most of the modernistic high-rise flats in the Bijlmer were still empty at the beginning of the 1970s.

24 In the Bijlmer, urban planners wanted to create a Modernist ideal for the citizens: 'spacious, sunny high-rise homes for a happy family life amidst a green, park-like landscape in which to relax and play.' G. Mak, 'Amsterdam as the "Compleat Citie": A City Plan read in Five Episodes', in: S. Musterd and W. Salet (eds.), *Amsterdam Human Capital* (Amsterdam: Amsterdam University Press, 2003) 31–48

Supported by governmental subsidies, the area drew low-income residents, a majority of whom were immigrants from Suriname, a former Dutch colony that became independent in 1975. More than 50 percent of the new tenants, many of whom had just arrived in the country, were unemployed when they moved to the neighbourhood that was devoid of any social and cultural facilities. As a result, the abundant space the development promised became not a green idyll, but a vast and unsafe public space, punctuated by Corbusian housing blocks.

From the 1990s, major plans were drawn up to redevelop the area which by this point had acquired the reputation of a disadvantaged neighbourhood. Proposals included demolishing a majority of the high rises and upgrading others; changing and updating infrastructure; and above all, attracting new residents. The K-Neighbourhood was also included in this overhaul, and a programme of urban regeneration began in the early 2000s. However, the global financial crisis of 2008 swiftly put this process on hold, leaving large areas incomplete. Among them was an empty space right in the middle of the redevelopment, surrounding the Kraaiennest metro station. By 2016 and with new housing production high on the agenda, the municipality was ready to pick up development of the area again. However, unhappy residents insisted that the city's approach was too narrowly focused on housing development and not enough on the socio-economic issues of the area. This was exemplified, according to some residents, by the lack of attention to public space in the official plans. In particular, they criticized the absence of ideas for a new central square for the neighbourhood. A well-organized neighbourhood group – Heart for the K-Neighbourhood – was successful in lobbying the municipality to start an extensive participatory trajectory to improve the plans and realize an inclusive public space.

In 2018, after almost a year of participatory meetings the group withdrew support from the outcomes of the participation trajectory. It claimed that the process had not only focused insufficiently on social aspects of the public space, but also failed to fully reach out to the community. Within the civic group resident Mike Brantjes, a newcomer to the K-Neighbourhood, took on the role of community organizer and social innovator to scrutinize the power relations inherent in the participation process with the government. When residents wanted to alter the rules of this urban process and formulated their own changes to the existing planning scheme, the city was unwilling to accommodate these requests. It turned out that the city's planning department only accepted input from residents if it was within the confines of their predefined urban planning processes. It was only when the Heart for the K-Neighbourhood organized a so-called 'participation strike' to show the municipality that rather than push their own plans, they needed to listen that the government finally changed course. Instead of executing plans as they had been drawn up within this rather rigidly top-down steered urban regeneration project, the city government put the execution of the urban development plans to a halt.

Through a change of city government and a greater focus on democratization, the Heart for the K-Neighbourhood was finally granted the right to start up the participation process again and contribute to the developments in their neighbourhood. As such, the renewed cooperation to define the urban plans shifted from a top-down process to a grassroots one. Before the civic initiative was granted a budget for their leading role in the drafting of the urban development plan, the district council made a try-out with a test case. Using a budget of 610,000 Euros from the city's Developing Neighbourhood programme assigned in 2018, Heart for the K-Neighbourhood had to prove their trustworthiness to represent the community's wishes for which objects and functions to add in the public space. In this first trial, the neighbourhood group consulted other community groups and difficult-to-reach residents for input of the public space design. With more than 117 ideas, they then decided together with the municipality which needs of the residents to accommodate. With their budget they were able to put up two-thirds of the submissions ranging from park bench designs to better street lighting – proving to the city and district council that they were able to operate on the behalf of their neighbourhood.

Eventually in 2019, the Heart for the K-Neighbourhood became an active stakeholder in the urban regeneration project, advising the municipality how the area should take shape. To execute this cooperative way of working for finalizing the urban development plan, the municipality as well as the civic initiative wanted to formalize their tasks and authorities within a social contract. When negotiating the details of the contract, municipal lawyers had difficulties in making it legally feasible within the framework of the municipality of Amsterdam: as juridical experts they wanted to foresee all eventualities within the contract agreements. This led to mistrust and irritation among the civic stakeholders. To realize some binding agreements, they finally decided to set up an agreement of intent within the framework of the municipality of Amsterdam. Legally less strict, the document allows both parties to lay down their commitments.[25]

A remaining sensitive point within these negotiations for a social contract was proper remuneration for the civic initiative's participatory work. Out of principal, the municipality did not want to compensate citizens involved in participation projects; to do so would set a precedent. Only when the role of the Heart for the K-Neighbourhood was underscored as one contributing to process development, and more involved than simply discussing plans within an ordinary participation project, did officials agree to reserve financial remuneration. Finally, the civic participants were acknowledged by the municipality as neighbourhood professionals, and a budget of 190,000 Euros was made available for compensating their expertise within the planning process.[26]

The question that is repeatedly put forth within this joint effort to develop this area is: What kind of neighbourhood does the K-Neighbourhood want to be? For whom will the place be designed? Both the municipality and the neighbourhood group want to demonstrate that urban development can be done differently, and that residents should have an active role and say. However, there are significant stumbling blocks to overcome. The case of the K-Neighbourhood shows that disruption of municipality-initiated participative urban development can lead to changes in the city's urban planning schemes. Anecdotally, this process also demonstrated that there is still little willingness among civil servants to work on such participatory projects. Translating civic needs into urban plans requires extensive negotiation, flexibility, and above all, patience among administration as well as civil society. Whether this cooperation will come to a successful urban development plan awaits to be seen.

---

25 The 2020 letter of commitment, or *afsprakenbrief*, included the budget and tasks to be performed by the municipality and the civic initiative. H. Van den Hende, I. Nio, K. de Nijs and S.J. H. Majoor, 'K-buurt: er is leven na de participatiestaking', in: J. N. Van Aanholt (ed.) *Participatiedilemma's* (Amsterdam: Hogeschool van Amsterdam, 2021), 12-17

26 H. Van den Hende, I. Nio, K. de Nijs and S.J.H. Majoor, 'K-buurt: er is leven na de participatiestaking', op. cit. (note 25), 16.

Intermediary Practice of Cooperation and Negotiation

The earlier mentioned cultural institution Pakhuis de Zwijger makes for an interesting study in its own right regarding the theme of this chapter. Illustrative of an initially bottom-up civic initiative that was then embraced by the government, it is a showcase example of Amsterdam's Creative Industry Policy. As a cultural venue, the former squat serves the needs of citizens, businesses and the city administration alike and brings together a range of stakeholders from government to residents to steer urban developments from the grassroots. Through its 'Amsterdam Approach' initiative, which brings together citizens, the private sector and government, Pakhuis de Zwijger played an important intermediary role in both Buiksloterham and the K-Neighbourhood.

A recent example of its informal political standing was the government's 2019 *Agenda Democratization,* presented at the cultural venue.[27] That saw Deputy Mayor Rutger Groot Wassink elaborate on a new policy focussed on giving more ownership to residents within citizen participation. Described as an 'experiment' that aims to explore new ways of cooperation for an inclusive city, the policy document underlined the necessary paradigm change within the city administration to one of 'test and try.'[28] One of the neighbourhood initiatives presented at the event was Heart for the K-Neighbourhood. In the aftermath of its 'participation strike,' their presence and involvement helped further future participation trajectory. In this and other cases, Pakhuis de Zwijger acted as a cultural and social broker between the government and citizens. As a cultural institution, it recruits new participants into the urban agenda, including civilians keen to engage with social and environmental issues in their respective neighbourhoods and establish projects. Specifically, a 'City Makers' initiative has furthered multilevel and multi-stakeholder cooperation between local government, civil society, communities, businesses and institutions, and contributed to the European Urban Agenda.[29]

---

27 Pakhuis de Zwijger. (2019). Presentatie Agenda Democratisering Amsterdam : Coöperatief Amsterdam. Available at: https://www.youtube.com/watch?v=KdFFIOSgb4M (21 April 2021)
28 R. Groot Wassink, *Democratisering*. Amsterdam [Letter of government, 19 March 2019], Gemeente Amsterdam, 2.
29 European Commission (2016) Urban Agenda for the EU: Pact of Amsterdam, Amsterdam.

Though Pakhuis de Zwijger initiates and facilitates discussions and dialogues between different interest groups and serves as a podium to question urban developments, it has also been criticized for its overly pragmatic approach. Partially financed by the City of Amsterdam itself, the cultural initiative has incorporated a slick language of problem solving discourses: it considers social and economic problems in the city as 'design challenges' or 'opportunities for innovative business models' — rather than as major social issues that ask for substantive debates and possibly radical policy changes.[30] At the same time, diverse citizen initiatives use the platform as a podium to discuss development of their neighbourhoods, as well as other urban and social developments. In doing so, they effectively work with an organization that is supported by the city itself — that is, people who 'belong' to the institutional and political parties they have been struggling with or fighting against.

Conclusion: Struggling for a Balance

The changing alliances between government, private stakeholders and civil society that we saw in Buiksloterham, the K-neighbourhood and Pakhuis de Zwijger are integral to a typical Amsterdam approach. That is to say: conflicts and protests are integrated, discussed, and often co-opted through the interplay of civic and private institutions for a consensus-driven solution. As the case studies show, Amsterdam's citizens find themselves in an uneasy relationship with their government concerning participative urban planning: for the most part, residents have not yet been treated as serious partners. Though the rhetoric of the municipality of Amsterdam in the development process has changed into an 'enabling' role in the last decade, mediating between civil actors and market parties, the degree of participation has – for a big part – not yet been impressive. Applying Sherry Arnstein's ladder of citizen participation from 1969, citizen participation in Amsterdam seems heavy on the first two steps – 'manipulation' and 'informing' – and much less in the highest ones ('direct decision making' and 'co-production'). This could explain why a bottom-up initiated platform such as Pakhuis de Zwijger has been so readily embraced by the city government and citizens alike: it serves as an informal political arena for discussions on the cooperative development of the city and the use of the public domain. Within the Eigenlogik of Amsterdam it

30 S. Olma, 'Ideology and the city: De Zwijger as an-aesthetic interface', *Amsterdam Alternative* (6 May 2019). Online. Available HTTP: https://amsterdamalternative.nl/articles/7486

functions as a buffer zone for informal negotiations between a strong government and an active, but not always empowered, civil society.

The involved citizens in Buiksloterham belong to groups who know who to address and network with. Generally speaking, they tend to be self-employed, educated, male and white. In the K-Neighbourhood, a majority of residents are of an immigrant background, and tend to be low paid. The latter group needed an incentive from a person from outside to feel entitled to pursue their rights. In founding the citizen initiative Heart for the K-Neighbourhood they established the formal tools to contest the imbalance of power between the government administration and themselves. Despite being recognized as professionals — in the case of Buiksloterham, in sustainability and circularity; and in K-Neighbourhood for their expert insights into their own locale — citizens have not yet secured lasting impacts on the underlying mechanisms of participatory urban development.

For a more balanced and possibly more productive future between a strong government and vocal citizenry there are still questions to address. First: are politicians and civil servants up to engaging with a more time-consuming and adaptive participatory way of development? Do you need a 'civic professional' to take the leadership role for a citizen group like in the K-Neighbourhood? And how can current underlying 'business models' of urban development be adapted? As Amsterdam's current 'experiments' show, there is still much to be absorbed into the city's urban planning system. Throughout its history, Amsterdam's strong government has incorporated bottom-up forces into its policy, giving some space to an empowered civil society to steer developments themselves. Herein lies the Eigenlogik that has brought the city prosperity and acclaim — but that also demands continual maintenance, struggle, realignment and care.

Bibliography

Arnstein, S. R., 'A Ladder of Citizen Participation', *Journal of the American Planning Association* (1969) 85(1), 24–34

Bredewold, F., Duyvendak, J.W., Kampen, T., Tonkens, E., and Verplanke, L., *De verhuizing van de verzorgingsstaat* (Amsterdam: Van Gennep, 2018)

Bureau Broedplaatsen, *Revised Studio and Creative Incubator Policy for Amsterdam 2015-2018* (2016), Amsterdam

Dembski, S., Case study Amsterdam Buiksloterham, the Netherlands: the challenge of planning organic transformation', (CONTEXT Report; No. 2). (Amsterdam: University of Amsterdam, AISSR programme group Urban Planning, 2013)

Duivenvoorden, E., *Een voet tussen de deur: Geschiedenis van de kraakbeweging 1964-1999* (Amsterdam, Antwerpen: Uitgeverij De Arbeiderspers, 2000)

European Commission, *Urban Agenda for the EU: Pact of Amsterdam* (2016), Amsterdam

Fainstein, S., *The Just City* (Ithaca and London: Cornell University Press, 2010)

Faludi, A. and Van der Valk, A., *Rule and Order. Dutch planning doctrine in the Twentieth Century* (Dordrecht: Kluwer, 1994)

Feddes, F., *A Millenium of Amsterdam: Spatial History of a Marvellous City* (Bussum: THOTH Publishers, 2014)

GroenLinks *Werkgroep Democratisering | Amsterdam* (2019). Online. Available HTTP: https://amsterdam.groenlinks.nl/werkgroep-democratisering

Groot Wassink, R., *Democratisering*. Amsterdam [Letter of government, 19 March 2019], Gemeente Amsterdam

Heerma, E., Volkshuisvesting in de jaren negentig (Housing in the nineties), Second Chamber 1988-1989, 20.691 Nos. 2-3, The Hague: SDU, 27 April 1989

Jacobs, J., *The Death and Life of Great American Cities* (New York: Random House, 1961)

Jolles, A., Klusman, E. and Teunissen, B., *Stadsplan Amsterdam. Toekomstvisies op de ruimtelijke ontwikkeling van de stad* (Rotterdam: NAi, 2003)

Koolmees, T. and Majoor S.J.H., 'Local government in the face of crisis: Changing public management of urban projects in Amsterdam', in: Raco, M. and Savini, F. (eds.), *Planning and Knowledge: How new forms of technocracy are shaping contemporary cities* (Bristol: Policy Press, 2019) 59-73

Lefebvre, H. (1968) 'The Right to the City: Philosophy of the City and Planning Ideology', *Atlas of Places*, Essay XXIV

Mak, G., 'Amsterdam as the "Compleat Citie": A City Plan read in Five Episodes', in S. Musterd and W. Salet (eds.), *Amsterdam Human Capital* (Amsterdam: Amsterdam University Press, 2003) 31–48

Metabolic, Studioninedots, and DELVA Landscape Architects, *Circular Buiksloterham: Transitioning Amsterdam to a Circular City: Vision & Ambition.* (Amsterdam: Circular Buiksloterham, 2015). Online. Available HTTP: https://buiksloterham.nl/project/1301/living-lab-en-manifest--rapport--report

Milikowski, F., *Van wie is de stad?: De strijd om Amsterdam* (Amsterdam, Antwerpen: Atlas Contact, 2018)

Needham, B., *Dutch Land-use Planning. The principles and the practice* (Farnham, Ashgate, 2014)

Olma, S., 'Ideology and the city: De Zwijger as an-aesthetic interface', *Amsterdam Alternative* (6 May 2019). Online. Available HTTP: https://amsterdamalternative.nl/articles/7486

Pruijt, H., 'Squatters in the Creative City: Rejoinder to Justus Uitermark', *International Journal of Urban and Regional Research* (2004) 28(3), 699–705

Savini, F., Boterman, W.R., Van Gent, W.P.C. and Majoor, S.J.H., 'Amsterdam in the 21st century: Geography, housing, spatial development and politics', *Cities* (2016) 52, 103-113

Savini, F. and Dembski, S., 'Manufacturing the Creative City: Symbols and Politics of Amsterdam North', *Cities* (2016) 55, 139–147

Stapper, E. W., Van der Veen, M., and Janssen-Jansen, L. B., 'Consultants as intermediaries: Their perceptions on citizen involvement in urban development', *Environment and Planning C: Politics and Space* (2020) 38(1), 60–78

Stephens, M., 'The Fiscal Role of the European Union: The Case of Housing and the European Structural Funds', *Urban Studies* (1999) 36(4), 715–735

Twist, M. van, Chin-A-Fat, N., Scherpenisse, J., and Steen, M. van der (eds.), *'Ja, maar...': Reflecties op de participatiesamenleving* (Den Haag: Boom Lemma, 2014)

Uitermark, J., 'An in memoriam for the just city of Amsterdam', *City* (2009) 13(2–3), 347–361

Van der Cammen, H. and De Klerk, L.A., *The Selfmade Land. Culture and evolution of urban and regional planning in the Netherlands* (Houten: Het Spectrum, 2012)

Van der Geyn, B. and Draaisma, J., 'The embrace of Amsterdam's creative breeding ground', in: Porter, L. and Shaw, K. (eds.), *Whose Urban Renaissance? An international comparison of urban regeneration strategies* (London and New York: Routledge, 2009) 202-211

Van den Hende, H., Nio, I., Nijs, K. de, & Majoor, S.J.H., 'K-buurt: er is leven na de participatiestaking', in: J. N. Van Aanholt (ed.), *Participatiedilemma's* (Amsterdam: Hogeschool van Amsterdam, 2021)

Van Hooijdonk, C., *De relevantie van het Amsterdamse Broedplaatsenbeleid anno 2010* (Utrecht: Universiteit Utrecht, 2010)

GRONINGEN

EM2
oosterhofholman

By Invitation Only

Citizen Participation in Groningen

Wendy Tan, Melika Levelt, Mustafa Hasanov and Peter Bootsma

Having endured benign neglect from the central government and general disdain from the rest of the country, Groningen has developed into a tenacious and self-reliant town where citizens are increasingly engaged with shaping and transforming their city. This chapter illustrates the *eigenlogik* of Groningen and its citizens through two recent yet decidedly different community-led initiatives, set against a historical backdrop of urban planning projects. Citizen participation here has changed drastically since the 1960s as a result of political change and larger societal transitions. More recently, following the 2008 financial crisis Groningen has seen a rash of initiatives with varying levels of citizen participation. In response, the city's local government has adapted its approach to facilitate and 'invite' participation. Critically reflecting on the narratives and power structures behind the initiatives described, this chapter discusses the discrepancies between levels of participation and concludes that although the city is welcoming to initiatives, the boundaries and thresholds to citizen participation remain opaque.

A Jewel with a Golden Edge: Groningen

'*Er gaat niets boven Groningen*' — 'There is nothing above Groningen' — is the motto of the northern-most region of the Netherlands and the location of an eponymous province and city. This highly successful marketing slogan has been used heavily in city branding for the last 30 years, and can be found splashed across buildings, hot air balloons and a wealth of merchandise sold in tourist information kiosks throughout Groningen. As most things in this city, the phrase is open to interpretation and ambiguity. On the one hand, it is part proclamation of excellence: although home to just 200,000 inhabitants, Groningen is the economic motor of the three most northern provinces of the Netherlands, and home to one of the country's oldest universities that counts four Nobel prize winners among its alumni. Simultaneously, it is a derogatory allusion to the fact that once you move northwards from the city, urbanization and settlements are displaced by a sparsely populated, flat and empty rural landscape. It speaks to the character of the city and the region that inhabitants have 'leaned into' the slogan and its implications of identity as a badge of honour.

This contrary stance is captured in the sentiments of its inhabitants in how they view themselves as 'other' in relation to the rest of the Netherlands. Even on a regional level, the 'true' locals prefer to be called *Stadjers* — or city folk — as opposed to the more common *Groninger* attributed to inhabitants of the surrounding countryside. Expanding further outwards still, residents also set themselves apart from those that reside in the economic centres of the Randstad in the West. This denigration of being a 'westerner' does not discriminate and includes everyone from policy makers in the Hague to anyone who lives outside of the Netherlands' three northern-most provinces.[1] In the Groningen region, there is a deep-seated and at times justified distrust and aversion to central authority and policies. The inhabitants have been repeatedly subjected to what they consider as unfair policies and depictions by those outside of the North. The 'northerners' are usually portrayed as being slow-witted, boorish, as having an unintelligible local dialect, and contentious in popular media.[2] The resentment and sense of being left behind is not baseless. In comparison to other parts of the country, the infrastructure development in the region has consistently lagged behind. The induced earthquakes from natural gas harvesting in the region has also devastated many historical settlements with almost none of the economic profits returning to the inhabitants.[3] As a result, there is a sense of pride among inhabitants in being resilient and self-sufficient, despite being dealt a poor hand in their geographical

---

1 W. Joustra, 'Kabinet neemt Noorden eindelijk weer serieus', *De Volkskrant*, 18 April 1998. Online. Available HTTP: https://www.volkskrant.nl/nieuws-achtergrond/kabinet-neemt-noorden-eindelijk-weer-serieus~b0838735/ (Last accessed: 21 Aug 2019)

2 'Noorderlingen gesloten en terughoudend', nu.nl, 2 April 2004. Online. Available HTTP: https://www.nu.nl/algemeen/301981/noorderlingen-gesloten-en-terughoudend.html (Last accessed: 21 Aug 2019); van der Galien, M. (2020) Groningers woest over windmolengekte: 'Den Haag ziet ons als dom volk. Een wingewest'. *De Dagelijkse Standaard* (08 October 2020). Available via: https://www.dagelijksestandaard.nl/2020/10/groningers-woest-over-windmolengekte-den-haag-ziet-ons-als-dom-volk-een-wingewest/ [Last accessed: 21 Nov 2020]

3 M.M. Bakema, C. Parra, P. McCann, 'Analyzing the Social Lead-Up to a Human-Induced Disaster: The Gas Extraction-Earthquake Nexus in Groningen, The Netherlands', *Sustainability* (2018) 10(10), 3621

situation. Simply, they successfully take care of their own in spite of a lack of support from the central government.

Grunnegs Ontzet: Groningen Defiance and Innovation

The city and the region carry the burden of playing second fiddle to the economic powerhouse cities in the west of the country. The city and its people are often portrayed as recalcitrant and slow to conform to national policies.[4] However, they have also been described as independent freethinkers who are unwilling to bend to the pressures of central authority, and who have succeeded both historically and in current times in forging their own path forward. A controversial infrastructure plan spanning the last three decades reflects this uncomfortable position: the *Zuiderzeelijn* is a high-speed rail extension aimed at improving train speed and frequency in the North and connecting it to the main national airport, Schiphol, and the west of the country. The project has been dangled in front of inhabitants since the late 1980s in return for the exploitation of natural gas reserves. The plan was eventually cancelled citing 'too high' costs. Nevertheless, it occasionally resurfaces in policy documents and in the media (usually around election time) to spark hope that the North will somehow catch up with the West someday.

It is no coincidence that the most prominent celebration in the city is not any of the traditional Dutch holidays one would expect. Rather, it is *Grunnegs Ontzet*: an explosive evening of fireworks and revelry in late August celebrating the 1672 relief of the city by its common citizens resisting the siege led by a bishop known as *Bommen Berend*. The city celebrates its independence proudly, and has always been a little bit ahead of its time in dancing to a different tune than the rest of the country. Politically, the local government was a stronghold of socialist democracy, with the Labour party dominating politics for decades since the 1970s, even when

---

4 R. van Meurs, 'Hoe een onhandigheidje van een minister tot een booming economie in het noorden leidde', *B&G* (May/June 2003). Online. Available HTTP: https://www.bngbank.nl/BG%20Articles/200306meurs_14-19.pdf (Last accessed: 21 Aug 2019); A-L. van Bruaene, 'Groningen, a city apart. The past to modern times of a stubborn city (1000-1600)', *Tijdschrift voor Geschiedenis* (2008) 121(1), 109-110

national politics tended towards conservatism.[5] This has changed in recent years when they were replaced by a social liberal party in 2014, and the Green party in 2018. The same socialist democratic political sentiments are also reflected in the city's urban development evolution. A particular turning point was the 1973 decision to demolish the Harmonie building. A cultural centre built in 1856 with a concert hall famed for its acoustic qualities, years of neglect had left the venue in a state of decline. Going against popular opinion, the city council decided to demolish the building and relocate its cultural activities. Amidst protest over the rigid handling of its demolition, a call for citizen participation arose.[6] In the 1970s, when a young and progressive Labour party bloc came into power, it pushed a radical but innovative framework to remake the city centre and give voice to citizens as the newly elected city council. Amongst other innovations, the proposed traffic circulation plan introduced unprecedented pedestrianization, prioritized bicycle traffic and kept private cars out of the city. This is now the norm in most European cities, but four decades ago, it raised incredible ire from local business owners and residents. However, looking back, the experimental plans did eventually deliver a vibrant and vital urban centre that has been repeatedly crowned as the top cycling city in the country of cycling culture.[7]

The Emperors of Zuiderdiep: Engaging the Citizenry

Since the voluminous criticism of the lack of citizen participation in the 1960s, the city has evolved in its approaches to engage the citizenry. In the past decades, the chief civil servant of the planning department has been nicknamed the 'Emperor of the Zuiderdiep' (*de Keizer van het Zuiderdiep*) by local residents, after the street where the department is located. The pejorative typecasts the overbearing planners and politicians who reinvented the city without much oversight from stakeholders, or consultation. Even though improvement efforts were made, the following projects illustrate that despite citizen participation in urban development evolving over time, there was and is still much ground to be won.

---

5 S. Tsubohara, *Democracy through Political Parties and Public Participation: The Case of the Planning History of Groningen, The Netherlands* (Groningen: URSI, 2010)

6 L.H. Hajema, *De glazenwassers van het bestuur: lokale overheid, massamedia, burgers en communicatie, Groningen in landelijk perspectief 1945-2001*, (Groningen: Rijksuniversiteit Groningen, 2001), 447; B. de Vries, 'Politiek en bestuur in spannende jaren', in: M. Duijvendak and B. de Vries (eds.) *Stad van het Noorden: Groningen in de twintigste eeuw* (Assen: Van Gorcum, 2003), 258 – 259

7 J.R. Homrighausen and W.G.Z. Tan, 'Institutional Innovations for Sustainable Mobility: Comparing Groningen (NL) and Phoenix (US)', *Transportation Research Procedia* (2016) 19, 151–163

The Groninger Museum planned in the mid 1980s resulted in heated debate. Using every means possible, citizens protested its location, design, and choice of architect. The entire process echoed a common refrain: the populace was being ignored, and decisions were being made behind closed doors by a political inner circle and an idiosyncratic museum director.[8] This continued in to the late 1990s with the Grote Markt: the central market square where the city hall and Martini church is located. It functions as a social and identifiable centre of the medieval part of the city and hosts weekly markets. When plans were mooted to renovate the buildings and introduce an underground parking garage, a farce of a referendum was held with one plan and no alternatives. Despite negative votes for the parking garage, the municipality saw no reason to deviate from their solitary plan.[9] As a result of the frustrations that ensued, citizen participation started to show teeth. Citizens, shop owners and civil servants managed to torpedo the top-down approved Regiotram project by expressing their negative sentiments via social media "worsened with the rise of Twitter" to oppose the project as an organized collective.[10]

Up until the early 2000s, citizen participation in Groningen stagnated at the informing and consultation phases. At best, it showed degrees of tokenism at the lower rungs of Arnstein's 1969 ladder of citizen participation. Referendums, albeit with restricted choices and only token engagement of citizens seemed par for the course. Despite the socialist democratic tendencies of the local government, the engagement of citizens, particularly in urban planning processes, could be described as paternalistic at best — and patronizing at worst.

By Invitation Only: Urban Planning and Citizen Participation

The last decade has signalled a shift in the engagement of citizenry to participate in urban development processes in Groningen. Under the auspices of the Recovery Act (*Crisis-en herstelwet*) introduced in 2010, the principles of planning by invitation (or '*uitnodigingsplanologie*') became a mainstay narrative in urban planning in many Dutch cities. Groningen was no exception.

The neighbourhood participatory budgets proposed in the mid 2000s demonstrated how the local government wanted to engage citizens at a much earlier

---

8 Hajema, *De glazenwassers van het bestuur*, op. cit. (note 6)

9 de Vries, 'Politiek en bestuur in spannende jaren', op. cit. (note 6), 437

10 R. van der Bijl, K. Utsunomiya and N. van Oort, 'Failed Projects Offer Valuable Lessons for Future Schemes', *International Railway Journal* (2020) 60(2), 34–37

stage in the development process. With an aim of instilling self-organization and governance at a neighbourhood level, the New Local Accords policy (*Nieuwe Lokaal Akkord*) was to allocate €20 million over four years to 14 neighbourhoods. A selected and nominated group of residents worked together with professionals to form a neighbourhood team (*wijkteam*) and make plans together with local government representatives on how best to spend their neighbourhood budgets on social and physical infrastructures. The teams were accountable only to the city council (Gemeente Groningen, 2008).[11] This marked a big step in putting both resources and decision-making powers in the hands of local inhabitants. However, preliminary evaluations reveal that it was mostly professional representatives leading decision-making due to a lack of capacity of the residents. .[12]

A key turning point was in 2015, when a group of citizens got financial and organizational support from the city to launch a G1000 dialogue — a citizen initiative for a deliberative collective of 1,000 citizens developed in Belgium by cultural historian, archaeologist and writer, David van Reybrouck. The citizens, chosen via lottery, were to gather to discuss the issues that they see as most important for their city. After a day's deliberation, they then decide on ten projects to make the city better. In Groningen the G1000 was run by volunteers who wore multiple hats as community organizers and civil servants. Ideas spanning universal basic income to a map of community-led initiatives were discussed, although the forum did not have any formal effect on policies. The event is seen by most as an opening-up of local government towards more involvement of citizen participation processes in the form of community-led initiatives.[13] These initiatives are led or initiated by self-organized groups of citizens and stakeholders within a defined community. More recently, with the introduction of district teams (*gebiedsteams)*; social welfare and communication teams at district levels (*WIJ-teams*); plus a how-to guide for citizen participation, the city is gaining traction in becoming more inclusive and transparent about their processes.

Prior to 2010, and despite good intentions, citizenry engagement in Groningen was characterized by its almost 'paternal' concern. That is to say, one party had a

11 Gemeente Groningen, *Rapportage Nieuw Lokaal Akkoord*, 2008

12 A. Michels, 'Citizen participation and democracy in the Netherlands', *Democratization* (2006) 13(2), 323–339

13 A. Michels and H. Binnema, 'Hoe divers, invloedrijk en deliberatief is een G1000?: Het ontwerp van een burgertop en de verwezenlijking van democratische waarden', *Bestuurswetenschappen* (2016) 70(1)

care-taking role; the other needed caring for. The imbalance of these roles was a clear signal of unequal footing. After a move towards more community-led initiatives, kickstarted by the 2015 G1000, citizen engagement in the city fell more in line with the contemporary narratives of deliberative democratic policies accompanying governmental devolution at both national and EU levels. There is an implicit acknowledgement that there is capacity within the citizenry to contribute more to correct market (and perhaps policy) failures. Here, a more collaborative stance is taken as opposed to that of the previous decade. This can be considered as moving up Arnstein's ladder of participation towards the beginnings of citizen control beyond tokenism. However, the term 'invitation' implies citizens and their initiatives are guests bound by the necessary etiquette and societal norms of decency within a host's domain.

The two stances beg the question: just how welcome is citizen participation in Groningen? And what are its boundaries and thresholds beyond formalistic referendums which may get ignored; or experimental budgets dominated by professionals instead of local citizens? Within this context, we discuss two vastly different community-led initiatives that show the range of justifications given in support of — and that go against — certain initiatives, and the resulting limits for participation.

Community-Led Initiatives in Groningen

The city and region of Groningen is drowning in community-led initiatives and projects due to the independence of its citizens and the regulatory permissiveness of the local government, particularly for achieving energy transition.[14] Initiatives vary from urban farms (such as Tuin in de Stad and Toentje) and energy co-ops (Grunneger Power); to social cooperatives (like Helpman-de Wijert, which sees students, residents, entrepreneurs and the municipality work together on neighbourhood projects) and large-scale urban transformation sites (such as mixed-use developments, Ebbingekwartier and Suikerfabriekterrein). They are found in every neighbourhood and range in size from a block-sized garden to a 40-hectare urban district.

14 M. Hasanov and C. Zuidema, 'The transformative power of self-organization: Towards a conceptual framework for understanding local energy initiatives in The Netherlands', *Energy Research & Social Science* (2018) 37, 85–93

One of the largest examples of this is the Ebbingekwartier, an urban redevelopment project on a former industrial site with a wealth of turn-of-the-century industrial heritage buildings, right in the heart of the city centre. Ebbingekwartier was revitalized by a group of local artists and entrepreneurs to discourage criminal and antisocial behaviour from taking place there. After years of clean-up and organizing cultural events staged in temporary shipping containers, the district was revived as a new hip spot of the city. The original initiative group was replaced by a more efficient managerial team appointed by the city. As the developers returned, all social and cultural value was eventually replaced by a highly desirable — but expensive — residential district.[15]

The growth of initiatives resulted from the urban development vacuum in the aftermath of the financial crisis of 2008. The halting and disappearance of development projects, coupled with a general financial downturn led to an increase in derelict locations and empty storefronts in and around the city of Groningen. On a positive note, citizens and their initiatives gained access to spaces and locations at peppercorn rates. However, as the real estate market started to bounce back after 2012, these sites also experienced extreme pressures to return to the status quo. Of course, not all initiatives are equally successful or resilient. Here, through the stories of two community-led initiatives that have transformed the spatial fabric or the existing processes within the city, we paint a picture of the spectrum of the city's recent culture of citizen participation. The first is a highly favoured initiative of an urban farm in the east quarter of the city; the latter is a less-favoured initiative seeking to improve older adult mobility in the north-west quarter of the city. Their narratives show the breadth of how cooperation between citizens and local government can manifest or deteriorate in planning processes.

Toentje

'Toentje' — or 'the little garden' in the local dialect — is an initiative in the Oosterpark neighbourhood, located east of Groningen's centre. The neighbourhood is a mix of 1930s labourer villages, bordered by post-war residential blocks and separated by green boulevards in the style of Berlage.[16] These are flanked by

15 K.C. von Schönfeld, W.G.Z. Tan, C. Wiekens, W. Salet and L. Janssen-Jansen, 'Social learning as an analytical lens for co-creative planning', *European Planning Studies* (2019) 27(7), 1291–1313

16 The father of modern architecture movement in the Netherlands, active in the early twentieth century. He famously used large green open spaces as structural key elements and axes in his plans to separate work and residential functions.

urban redevelopment projects from the late 2000s, left uncompleted due to the financial crisis. The area was notorious for the since-demolished local football stadium and its associations of overly fervent supporters, riots and extravagant firework displays come New Year's Eve. The neighbourhood is well-loved for its proximity to the city centre and two large parks, capped off by an Amsterdam-style building housing the local school. Now, it is home to a comfortable mix of lower socio-economic status families in a multitude of terraced social housing on the western edges of the Pioenpark; clusters of students in the rented post-war apartment blocks in the middle; and an influx of yuppies and their young families on the eastern edges in townhouses and luxury apartments.

Toentje developed in 2012 from a partial parcel of residential development (just under one hectare) left undeveloped due to the pressures of the financial crisis. It was not initiated by a local resident, but by a social entrepreneur with a professional background in event organization and music who was frustrated at the lack of fresh produce available to those in need. He approached the local municipality seeking a piece of ground to cultivate produce, specifically for the local food bank in the same neighbourhood. The initiative's clearly outlined plans (comprising mind maps and vision boards) of only producing for the food bank with a group of voluntary urban agricultural enthusiasts and a persuasive pitch caught the attention of several senior civil servants in the municipality. Together, a suitable location was found and the local residents consulted. The residents reacted positively as no one enjoyed looking at a piece of disheveled and bare ground awaiting construction that might never come to be. After a usage and lease agreement signed with the housing development corporation that owned the site in 2013, agricultural production went into full swing after a year of site preparation. The initiative formalized itself as a non-profit organization foundation in 2014, partially subsidized by the poverty prevention policies and budgets from the municipality. It went from strength to strength, attracting volunteers by the dozen who were seeking solace from work life stress, or an outlet for their green fingers. At one point, they had a rotation of more than 35 volunteers at any given time from all walks of life. Most, however, were young urban professionals from outside of the neighbourhood. Despite its successes, Toentje nevertheless faced hurdles: a first was when the foundation sought to branch into animal husbandry (pigs, chickens and so on) to increase the variety of produce and introduce circularity into its urban agriculture activities. This was met with protest from the residents due to potential smells, as well as those who were not looking forward to their children being confronted with an animal that they might consume.

As the real estate market recovered, Toentje was faced with its first crisis in 2015. With the lease agreement coming to an end, the development corporation wanted to regain the parcel of land to answer the rising demand for housing development. As the initiative sought potential new locations, they painstakingly tore down and packed up the garden they had cultivated for years. After a few months of searching, the initiative was eventually offered one of the green boulevards of the neighbourhood as a replacement site. The site had the appropriate zoning permissions and was only 100 metres away from the previous location. In its new location, which was cleared and prepared by the municipality, the garden once again flourished as part of the green structure of the neighbourhood. Without the fences of the old location, it also became more accessible. However, support from local residents did not come naturally. This pushed Toentje and the municipality to make considerable efforts to connect with the immediate neighbourhood. One reason for residents' initial dissatisfaction was that the neighbourhood desired a playground where Toentje now stood, as had been promised by the municipality long before the urban farm came into play. Starting with establishing links with the local school and municipal social workers, little by little, Toentje increased its connection with the local neighbourhood.

What then, if not a local connection, justified the municipal support of Toentje from the start? When interviewed, some civil servants praised the professionalism of the initiator, while others stated that Toentje fitted perfectly with multiple municipal policy goals. Certain policy makers saw Toentje's dependence on subsidies as problematic in the long run, as it should ultimately be able to operate commercially. Others disagreed, stating that the main idea of a citizen initiative is that it does not fit into any current framework for justification; rather it should achieve something new, and not yet thought of by the municipality. Thus, despite diverse views, a large variety of supportive justifications were given to the positive benefit of Toentje's continuation. However, as our next case study illustrates, such variety and variability of justifications can also work in opposition as boundaries and thresholds to citizen participation.

Vinkmobiel

Vinkmobiel is named after the neighbourhood in which it is based: Vinkhuizen, in the north-western edge of the city. A community initiative, it aims to provide alternative mobility solutions to the district's older adults in the form of a fleet of used electric golf vehicles (now replaced by cars due to weather conditions) that users can call up on demand for a small fee. The service was to be run by volunteers who are trained to be chauffeurs as part of a return to workforce training programme. The neighbourhood consists of apartment blocks dating from the 1970s and 1980s, and has all the typical ugliness of modern housing expansion schemes. This is seen in the unnecessarily wide roads that reduce walkability, lack of human scale, and abundance of high-rise flats of social housing in various states of disrepair. There is a local shopping centre with limited shops and facilities located near the only historical building, a barn that hosts the local community centre. The neighbourhood underwent transformation in the early 2000s, with the introduction of better housing quality. The aim of this was to attract a younger demographic of young professionals with families in order to balance out the increasingly ageing original residents belonging to lower socio-economic groups. Surprisingly, the neighbourhood is also very attractive to students due to its proximity to the local university.

In recent years, Vinkhuizen has suffered from governmental budget reductions in the aftermath of the financial crisis. These cuts are most visible in the reduction of bus services and stops within the neighbourhood. Here, the percentage of older adults exceeds the average for the municipality. 20 per cent of residents are aged 65 years and over, compared to the average of 12 per cent.[17] As such, this group of residents was disproportionately disadvantaged when bus lines were reduced and bus stops removed. Social workers and local community health care workers reported increasing cases of social isolation, exacerbating physical and mental health decline in the older adult population. Many were no longer able to visit friends, the hairdressers, or weekly markets in the city centre as bus lines were cancelled. In reaction, in 2014 the local community centre and healthcare provider proposed an initiative to facilitate short-distance trips for this vulnerable group. Limited to journeys of up to six kilometres — so as not to rival taxi companies — the project was inspired by similar schemes running in the south and east of the country. The initiative was initially met by warm responses from the local municipality, even securing praise and political support from multiple politicians. However, in seeking to secure subsidy during a city council meeting, the initiators discovered that favour from multiple fronts led to their proposal being considered unfeasible, politically sensitive and eventually denied. Dejected, the group behind the initiative disbanded, only to reunite the following year thanks to a local non-profit organization promoting sustainability through democratic processes, and

17 Centraal bureau voor de statistiek, 'Kerncijfers wijken en buurten 2019', *StatLine*. Available HTTP: http://data.overheid.nl/dataset/09f5479a-50f9-45ed-b727-91bf141d14f4 (accessed 21 August 2019)

mobility researchers from the local university. The initiative was subsequently involved in several EU and national funding proposals. Burned by prior rejections at a municipality level, they sought out alternative funding sources from the national lottery funds as well as other charity organizations. The group began formalizing their processes, specifically by laying down tasks and goals in a covenant as opposed to verbal agreements. Meetings were held more frequently as opposed to ad hoc and informal meet-ups between initiative members. Just as they gained traction by winning small subsidies from charities, they were tipped-off about a similar project also offering volunteer-run transportation in an adjacent neighbourhood. The group was devastated to see the very same organization that had rejected them — that is, the local municipality — implement their exact idea in a different location. This led to increased unpleasantness between the two parties. Eventually, in a reconciliation attempt, the group was offered a potential subsidy to implement their proposal on the condition that they further professionalized, and produced a viable business case. In the meantime, the group lost their transport operator who over the course of three frustrating years had grown impatient at the lack of progress, and resistance from local government.

The very next year, a social entrepreneur and regional car-leasing company stepped in to help fill that role. Their approach of commercialization, broadening the initiative's reach to multiple neighbourhoods, all the while retaining low fees was initially met with positive reactions from the municipality. However, on presentation of the business case questions were raised by the same civil servants as to how embedded it was in the local community. Promises of subsidies dissipated; the initiative was deemed too professional and therefore illegitimate. Having had enough, the initiative stopped requesting subsidies from local government and the transport operator established itself as a foundation, turning to grants secured from local banks and charities to start the project by purchasing vehicles. In 2019, Vinkmobiel launched with a fleet of six vehicles, with three more added in 2020. After overcoming early hiccups with its planning and booking processes, reactions from local (older adult) residents have been overwhelmingly positive.

Discussion and Conclusion

Looking back at the history of Groningen, one can see projects being shaped by various degrees of citizen participation. Across tools spanning formalistic consultations (*inspraak*) to referendums, the extent to which citizens have a say in their city continues to evolve. In the last decade, we see that the *Stadjer* have become increasingly vocal and more responsive in determining how the city should and could be. The city has also grown in giving space for alternative voices and processes by way of community dialogues and participatory budgets. However, as these case studies show, there are still implicit barriers for participation in Groningen that lead to an uneven playing field.

From Strength to Strength

The number of community-led initiatives popping up in Groningen has recently resulted in the creation of a democratic co-operative (*Burgerinitiatieven Gemeente Groningen* or BIG) where initiatives can organize, seek resources and support each other. The self-reported index stood at 180 initiatives at last count.[18] The city is home to a growing number of citizen participation in the form of community-led initiatives and projects. Judging by the number of initiatives reported, proactive citizen participation is definitely on the agenda. The local government has even recently produced a handbook on a Groningen style of citizen participation.[19] Thanks to efforts to introduce participatory budgets and local district officers' willingness to facilitate citizen participation, Groningen is one of the more advanced cities in the Netherlands. The political favour and support that Toentje experienced shows that the local governance structures are flexible and welcoming to the right kind of initiative. Vinkmobiel, although not as well-favoured, was not further obstructed: the initiative could proceed with its plans by piecing together the necessary financial resources independently.

Variety of Justication

Comparing the cases, the boundaries and thresholds for 'welcome' citizen participation through community-led initiatives remains opaque. It is not necessarily an issue of being place-based, being legitimized by the community, nor a matter of societal relevance or urgency. As an initiative from outside the neighbourhood, Toentje was well-loved and well-supported within the bureaucratic arenas of the local municipality. Vinkmobiel, on the other hand, an initiative of local stakeholders, was unsuccessful in gaining municipal appreciation. Both are still growing and how they will further develop is unclear. Perhaps like Ebbingekwartier, they might receive support up to the point when the initiatives are mature enough to

18 Burgerinitiatieven Groningen (BIG) (2020) Online. Available HTTP: https://burgerinitiatieven-groningen.nl/inventarisatie-burgerinitiatieven-2019/ (accessed 15 Apr 2021)
19 Gemeente Groningen, *Groninger Participatiewerkboek*, Gemeente Groningen: Groningen, 2019). Online. Available HTTP: https://gemeente.groningen.nl/sites/default/files/Groninger-Participatiewerkboek.pdf (accessed 21 Nov 2020)

be further exploited by market forces. Whilst the initiator of Toentje was praised for their professionalism, that same quality was first demanded and then mistrusted in the case of Vinkmobiel.

That the municipality is highly supportive of local initiatives is clear, and evidenced by the cross-disciplinary team of civil servants that takes care of a first examination of any initiative that demands support. However, the city's various means of justification seem intangible and oftentimes like a moving target. This creates a risk of arbitrariness influencing later decisions regarding support. As a favoured initiative, Toentje was afforded many conveniences and help such as entrance to subsidy budgets and preparation of the site. This is in stark contrast to another similar urban agricultural initiative in the city, Tuin in de Stad, which was required to demonstrate its economic and social value,[20] and of course Vinkmobiel that had to find other sources of funding to get started.

An Open Invitation?

Although the inability of the Vinkmobiel initiative to gain full support from all stakeholders might be construed as a failure, it can also be argued that the initiative overcame opposition to eventually realize its goals. A key difference here seems to be how 'inviting' an initiative was perceived to be. It might seem serendipitous for an initiative such as Toentje to receive support and facilitation. One could also argue that the initiators were more politically astute and knew how to present their ideas more efficiently to those in power, compared to the team behind Vinkmobiel. In this form of citizen participation, it is crucial to have and utilize community-organizing skill sets to achieve and sustain collective action for change.

Considering the tenacity and self-reliance of the city and its citizens, it is hardly surprising that there is capacity within the citizenry to challenge traditional norm of hierarchical and top-down planning decisions. The can-do attitude of inhabitants and willingness of the local government to experiment with varying degrees of citizen participation fits the identity of a city seeking self-sufficiency and excellence in retaliation. The trick, however, is that once the spotlight is turned onto the internal power structures within the city, a hierarchical pattern appears. The municipality is shedding its paternalistic ways of managing citizen participation

---

20 *Dagblad van het Noorden*, 'Tuin in de Stad moet verkassen', 9 September 2015. Online. Available HTTP: https://www.dvhn.nl/groningen/Tuin-in-de-Stad-moet-verkassen-21027156.html

— but is it enough to just be welcoming? The evidence points to intangible and changeable rules and norms about what is or is not welcomed by the hosts — the local government — that contrasts sharply with the city's history of non-conformity. Is it then that the guests — that is, the citizens and their community initiatives — are not able to behave as the hosts expect? This puts the onus of observing etiquette on citizens as new entrants into the developmental processes. One could question if such deference is societally desirable, given that the government should be a representation of its citizens. The very citizens that are in fact, correcting policy and market failures, and contributing time and resources to build societal value. After all, is it not the duty of the host to make their guests feel welcome by either expressing the rules beforehand or by graciously accepting all actions of their guests?

Bibliography:

Arnstein, S.R., 'A Ladder Of Citizen Participation', *Journal of the American Institute of Planners* (1969) 35(4), 216–224.

Bakema M.M., Parra, C. and McCann, P., 'Analyzing the Social Lead-Up to a Human-Induced Disaster: The Gas Extraction-Earthquake Nexus in Groningen, The Netherlands', *Sustainability* (2018) 10(10), 3621.

van der Bijl, R., Utsunomiya, K. and van Oort, N., 'Failed Projects Offer Valuable Lessons for Future Schemes', *International Railway Journal* (2020) 60(2), 34–37

van Bruaene, A-L., 'Groningen, a city apart. The past to modern times of a stubborn city (1000-1600)', *Tijdschrift voor Geschiedenis* (2008) 121(1), 109-110.

van der Galien, M. (2020) Groningers woest over windmolengekte: 'Den Haag ziet ons als dom volk. Een wingewest'. *De Dagelijkse Standaard* (08 October 2020). Available via: https://www.dagelijksestandaard.nl/2020/10/groningers-woest-over-windmolengekte-den-haag-ziet-ons-als-dom-volk-een-wingewest/ [Last accessed: 21 Nov 2020]

Gemeente Groningen. (2008). *Rapportage Nieuw Lokaal Akkoord*, Gemeente Groningen: Groningen. Hajema, L.H., *De glazenwassers van het bestuur: lokale overheid, massamedia, burgers en communicatie, Groningen in landelijk perspectief 1945-2001* (Groningen: Rijksuniversiteit Groningen, 2001) 447 p.

Hasanov, M. and Zuidema, C., 'The transformative power of self-organization: Towards a conceptual framework for understanding local energy initiatives in The Netherlands', *Energy Research & Social Science* (2018) 37, 85–93.

Homrighausen, J.R. and Tan, W.G.Z., 'Institutional Innovations for Sustainable Mobility: Comparing Groningen (NL) and Phoenix (US)', *Transportation Research Procedia* (2016) 19: 151–163.

van Meurs, R., 'Hoe een onhandigheidje van een minister tot een booming economie in het noorden leidde', *B&G* (May/ June 2003). Online. Available HTTP: https://www.bngbank.nl/BG%20Articles/200306meurs_14-19.pdf (Last accessed: 21 Aug 2019).

Michels, A. and Binnema, H. 'Hoe divers, invloedrijk en deliberatief is een G1000?: Het ontwerp van een burgertop en de verwezenlijking van democratische waarden', *Bestuurswetenschappen* (2016) 70(1).

Michels, A., 'Citizen participation and democracy in the Netherlands', *Democratization* (2006) 13(2): 323–339.

'Noorderlingen gesloten en terughoudend', *nu.nl*, 2 April 2004. Online. Available HTTP: https://www.nu.nl/algemeen/301981/noorderlingen-gesloten-en-terughoudend.html (Last accessed: 21 Aug 2019)von Schönfeld, K.C., Tan, W.G.Z., Wiekens, C., Salet, W. and Janssen-Jansen, L., 'Social learning as an analytical lens for co-creative planning', *European Planning Studies* (2019) 27(7): 1291–1313.

Tsubohara, S., *Democracy through Political Parties and Public Participation: The Case of the Planning History of Groningen, The Netherlands* (Groningen: URSI, 2010)W. Joustra, 'Kabinet neemt Noorden eindelijk weer serieus', *De Volkskrant*, 18 April 1998. Online. Available HTTP: https://www.volkskrant.nl/nieuws-achtergrond/kabinet-neemt-noorden-eindelijk-weer-serieus~b0838735/ (Last accessed: 21 Aug 2019)

de Vries, B., 'Politiek en bestuur in spannende jaren', in: Duijvendak, M. and de Vries, B. (eds.) *Stad van het Noorden: Groningen in de twintigste eeuw* (Assen: Van Gorcum, 2003) pp. 258 – 259

BERLIN

ALLESANDERSPLATZ
BÜHNEN

In Search of Berlin

A City Renegotiating Realities and Visions

Karin Christof and Franziska Sack

'Berlin is a city condemned always to become, never to be.'[1]

In his classic portrait, *Berlin, Ein Stadtschicksal* (1910), art critic and publicist Karl Scheffler – who came to Berlin from Hamburg in his twenties – delivered a verdict on the city's urban identity that has shaped its public image ever since. Literary flourishes aside, policy makers, politicians and urban planners still consider Scheffler's assessment a dynamic characteristic of the present-day capital of Germany that helps them realize urban developments. In this sense, the statement becomes not only a 'condemnation' but also a privilege and opportunity for the city's urban vision. In other words, Berlin never has to be, but can forever become.

As other cities worldwide, Berlin's current urban development is shaped by two major influences. On the one hand, economic interests have a strong impact on the development of the real estate and housing markets. At the same time, city planners of the municipal government, as well as a self-empowered civil society, strive to preserve the qualities of an inclusive city. In this field of tension, civil servants and citizen initiatives act to define guidelines, strategies and visions that serve a prosperous and just city, all the while seeking to position participation as key to its development.

1 K. Scheffler, *Berlin, Ein Stadtschicksal* (Berlin: Fannei & Walz,1989) 219: '*. . . Berlin dazu verdammt: immerfort zu werden und niemals zu sein.*'

The German capital markets itself as a place of stories to be told, and whose diversity of people – its Berliners – underpin its identity. This sentiment was reflected in the 2008 city branding campaign 'Be Berlin,' which also plays on Scheffler's 'forever to become' analysis.[2] But as well as painting the city as a place of unfolding possibilities and yet-to-be-defined narratives in a general sense, the notion could just as well apply to the city's current governance approach which positions civic engagement and participation as cornerstones of sustainable urban development. In this way, it alludes to the cultural-sociological concept of Berlin's possible intrinsic logic: the historic, cultural and economic changes that have inscribed themselves on the thinking and behaviour of a city's residents and have influenced how those cities developed. As such, cities can serve as 'entities of meaning' that contribute to and steer urban developments.[3]

Berlin's planning culture has been shaped repeatedly by civic engagement in urban planning processes. As demonstrated by several recent case studies, bottom-up, civilian-initiated approaches have long struggled for renewed forms of cooperation between governmental institutions, private parties and society at large. Nevertheless, cooperative urban developments in Berlin have had a major impact on the city's real estate politics – specifically with regard to the development of city- or state-owned land. Some, like non-profit cultural and community-focused initiative, the ExRotaprint project, are part upshot of the financial crisis of the mid-2000s; while others, such as mixed-use, concept-based development, Blumengroßmarkt, are the result of more recent economic changes.

Throughout Berlin's recent history – including German reunification, the financial crisis, as well as the city's emergence as an El Dorado of hipsters and artists at the beginning of the 2000s – the city has striven to keep pace with the evolving needs, preferences and identities of its residents. This ongoing quest for alignment in both urban development and participatory processes has enabled various forms of civic and public engagement.

---

2 Berlin Partner für Wirtschaft und Technologie GmbH (2008) *Be Berlin - die Hauptstadtkampagne*, https://be.berlin/beberlin/

3 M. Löw, 'The City as Experiential Space: The Production of Shared Meaning', *International Journal of Urban and Regional Research* (2013), vol 37, issue 3

A Brief Sequence of Events

Before diving into the different phases of civic engagement in urban renewal and regeneration projects from the 1970s until today, it is helpful to revisit some of the major political, cultural and economic influences of twentieth century geopolitical events on Berlin.

Berlin is a city-state with a polycentric lay-out and a de-concentrated city administration. While the city was the biggest in Europe in the roaring 1920s, it became a divided one after 1945. Separated by a 155-kilometre-long barrier, the Berlin Wall became the physical representation of the institutional divergence of two political systems. After the fall of the Wall in 1989, the reunification caused a territorial and administrative re-ordering. Not only was the Eastern local government and political system abolished and annexed after 40 years of division, spatially too, the two halves of the city had to be merged into one continuous urban entity. In this process, central and peripheral areas were redefined, and the focus of urban development questioned and turned upside down. Nevertheless, echoes of previously divided administrative structures can still be felt, and the city administration continues to operate in a fragmented way. In particular, the Senate tends to collide with the local District Offices concerning pressing issues such as new construction of housing or zoning of commercial areas.

In the early 1990s, the development of Berlin politics was based on assumptions of continuous growth of the total population, from 3.5 million up to 5 million. But the changes that had to be executed in government and administration; industrial decline and privatizations in East Berlin; as well as the discontinuation of subsidies for West and East Berlin all led to a serious long-term economic crisis for the city. Real estate politics was faced with the challenge of how to deal with vacant spaces and buildings. Nevertheless, this era is still regarded as a phase of great creative chaos and a maximum of freedom. Described as a 'legend of a chaotic, dirty and incredibly creative center' by *The New York Times*;[4] and famously as 'poor but sexy' by former Governing Mayor Klaus Wowereit in 2003 (a sound bite which fast became a leitmotif of the city), Berlin's perceived anarchy only

4 C. Schuetze, 'Looking Back to the '90s, When Berlin Was the Height of Cool,' *The New York Times*, 23 October 2018

increased the city's attractiveness. Still today, this narrative continues to resonate as an important driver for civic engagement in urban development.[5]

At the beginning of the new millennium, the city found itself again at deadlock. As the shrinking population reached its lowest in 2000, cuts to the administrative sector led to massive constraints in the operationality of the city of Berlin.[6] In 2001, several years before the global financial crisis hit, Berlin grappled with a home-made calamity of its own as the country's tenth-largest bank, public banking consortium *Bankgesellschaft Berlin*, plunged the German capital into debt through political corruption. For large parts of civil society, this represented a breach of public trust by an established institution that 'lost' several billion Euros of entrusted funds in risky loans for property investments. The majority city-owned bank forced the administration of Berlin to sell large portions of its housing property portfolio to close the deficit. From the beginning of the crisis until 2012, this totalled more than 6,300 real estate properties sold to private investors.[7] This massive sell-out of publicly owned land as well as communal infrastructure companies owned by the State of Berlin set a precedent and stage for contestations between civil society and the city state.

In the new millennium, the city has continued to attract young creatives in search of low living costs and a vibrant atmosphere. As a result, the city has become known for its busy start-up scene and thriving creative industries. By the beginning of 2020, Berlin had caught up economically with the rest of Germany and was no longer a capital poorer than the country itself.[8] In this sense, the city's policies have shown effect. To evoke the sound bite-turned-slogan coined by Wowereit once again, Berlin is (still) sexy – but not so poor anymore. In turn, the growing economy has led to a crisis of the housing market with a shortage of affordable apartments and rising rents. As a predicted population increase of more than 10

---

5 During the Covid 19 lockdowns of 2021, for example, posters outside closed bars read '*Ohne uns nur noch arm!*' ('Without us, simply poor!')

6 J. Paffhausen, *Bevölkerungsentwicklung Berlin* (Berlin: Amt für Statistik Berlin-Brandenburg, 2010). Online. Available HTTP: https://www.statistik-berlin-brandenburg.de/publikationen/aufsaetze/2010/HZ_201003-01.pdf

7 H. Prantl, 'Berlin ohne Grund und Boden,' *Blätter für deutsche und internationale Politik* – (October 2017) Online. Available HTTP: https://www.blaetter.de/ausgabe/2017/oktober/berlin-ohne-grund-und-boden

8 European Commission (2021), https://ec.europa.eu/growth/tools-databases/regional-innovation-monitor/base-profile/berlin

per cent by 2035 calls for infrastructural measures and policies,[9] the Senate has promised to realize an additional 194,000 dwellings by 2030.[10] Considering that Berlin is a city with a high percentage of tenants (85 per cent) versus homeowners, the need for rental supply from municipal housing corporations is particularly urgent. To realize affordable public-interest housing, the Senate has integrated half of its projected housing stock in the Urban Development Plan for Housing.[11] As part of that, the city-state has announced that it will activate its limited state-owned plots of land in a joint effort with all urban stakeholders including private parties, civil society and municipal agencies. The strategy follows the large-scale sell-off of land to speculative investors in the mid-2000s which saw the city's land ownership fall to just 40 per cent, and the subsequent acquisition of some of the same plots of land from private entities thereafter.

In the meantime, the economic growth of the city has led to an increase of land values that by 2018 saw them quadruple within the space of a decade.[12] This growth led to a doubling of rents in the free rental market, especially in inner-city locations. As the city of Berlin was only slowly taking action to respond to the lack of affordable housing, diverse parties including citizen groups, political bodies, and activists have protested against rapidly rising housing prices and the sell-out of the city's state-owned properties. From these entities, several significant urban demonstration movements and initiatives have emerged. Among them are *Mediaspree Versenken*, which protested the large-scale development of the Spree riverbank into a dedicated media quarter; citizen group *Stadt von Unten*, which was originally formed by residents of the *Dragoner Areal*, Kreuzberg in 2014 in objection to proposed privatization; and tenants' association *Kotti & Co*, also based in the southern borough of Kreuzberg and focused on the diverse neighbourhood around Kottbusser Tor.

The concerns of these citizen initiatives and groups span the gradual pushing out of middle- and lower-income groups; as well as the right to sustainable, affordable

---

9 P. Deschermeier, 'Bevölkerungsentwicklung in den deutschen Bundesländern bis 2035', *Institut der deutschen Wirtschaft Köln* (March 2018). Online. Available HTTP: https://www.iwkoeln.de/fileadmin/publikationen/2017/357919/IW-Trends_2017-03-04_Deschermeier.pdf

10 Senatsverwaltung für Stadtentwicklung und Wohnen (2019) *Stadtentwicklungsplan (SteP) Wohnen 2030*. Online. Available HTTP: https://www.stadtentwicklung.berlin.de/planen/stadtentwicklungsplanung/de/wohnen/index.shtml

11 Senatsverwaltung für Stadtentwicklung und Wohnen, *Stadtentwicklungsplan*, op. cit. (note 10)

12 E. Zimmer and K. Schoenecker *Entwicklung der Grundstücksverkäufe in Berlin und Brandenburg* (Berlin: Amt für Statistik Berlin-Brandenburg, 2019)

and inclusive housing. In 2018, at the height of the land speculation in Berlin, residents radicalized their fight for a more just city. Founding the initiative *Deutsche Wohnen & Co Enteignen,* multiple tenants' associations joined forces to demand a re-municipalization of some of the properties owned by large real-estate companies, including *Deutsche Wohnen.* In 2019, the group delivered a petition with more than 77,000 signatures demanding a legal transfer from private to public ownership for the purpose of nationalization. Signees supported a trade-off with the real estate companies: instead of exploiting existing (social) housing stock, they could instead invest in new real-estate projects. One outcome of the protest was Berlin becoming the first German state to operate a rent cap, or *Mietendeckel,* in 2020. Although still disputed in lawsuits, its proponents view the measure as the city taking responsibility for affordable housing conditions. Berlin residents and policy makers have long debated on which urban development strategies to follow. At the same time, experts have repeatedly voiced concerns at what they perceive as a lack of overall vision. This criticism is at odds with the ambitions that the city itself elaborated on in 2015 with collectively defined future-oriented strategy, the 'Berlin Strategy 2030.'[13] In its preface, Governing Mayor Michael Müller stated that the blueprint was the first to provide real guidance for how to sustainably develop the city since the German reunification in 1990. In this handbook for participation, the Senate of Berlin developed guidelines linked to practical examples for its administration to enable the implementation of participatory processes. The reality, however, has proven less straightforward: in the face of an enormous housing shortage, it is the economic forces of a tight land and real estate market that continue to dominate the debates surrounding implementation of these overall strategies. Criticism of the Senate's perceived shortcomings around new housing construction obstructs public discussion concerning future development of the city. The city administration often argues that participatory processes delay building projects, creating conflicts between public bodies and civil society that hinder the very participative efforts to cooperate.

13 Senate Department for Urban Development and the Environment et al., 2015

Berlin to Act: Civic Responses to the Recurring Housing Crisis

Rehab Squatting and Careful Urban Renewal

In the 1970s, the West German administration embarked on the strategic destruction of pre-war tenement blocks that were in a state of disrepair. Implementing urban renewal programmes, they realized new buildings instead of renovating them. The tenants who lived in these buildings protested their demolition, and joined forces with squatters who were occupying other vacant spaces.[14] Calling their activities rehab squatting and protesting the housing shortage as well as speculation in the city, squatters argued that it was 'better to squat and mend than to own and destroy.'[15] The mass protests were not only against politics of speculation, but also about the right to housing and desire for a more equitable – and affordable – urban sphere. The protesters called for a redistribution of housing and an immediate halt to the large-scale tabula rasa projects that destroyed valuable living spaces. Furthermore, they asked government to empower residents and enable self-organized housing, and realize democratically organized small-scale urban renewal to maintain mixed neighbourhoods.

Though squatters and tenants hoped to influence government policies, their demands initially found resonance in the progressive institutional testing field of the International Building Exhibition (IBA) in West Berlin. Established in 1901, this recurring exhibition format focuses on urban and regional development, and periodically strives to develop novel approaches to social issues and urban design ideas.[16] Model projects help to visualize and discuss politically controversial topics and aim to contribute to innovations within planning schemes. With a focus on new housing concepts, the 1979 international competition and expo sought solutions for new buildings in still empty areas around the city, as well as ways to implement small-scale urban renewal projects in demolished inner-city districts to safeguard and preserve the city as a viable mixed living space. Though

---

14 At the time there were at least 20,000 empty flats versus 50,000 people who needed a place to live. See A. Krüger, 'Local Communities and Urban Regeneration,' *Community Development Journal* (1993) vol 28, no, 4

15 The term rehab squatting, *instand(be)setzen*, is a portmanteau of the German terms for maintenance, *Instandsetzung*, and squatting, *Besetzung*. See A. Vasudevan, *The Autonomous City* (London and New York: Verso, 2013)

16 https://www.internationale-bauausstellungen.de/en/iba-history/

the projects realized within the IBA formats became no less susceptible to delays and red tape than any other urban development procedure, these innovative experiments have proven instrumental in creating participative and integrated planning processes that still apply today.

One such outcome of the IBA Berlin was that of 'careful urban renewal,' which was aimed squarely at the reconstruction of old buildings including self-help work of its occupants. By the 1990s, the city administration had incorporated the civic demands of these active citizen groups – constituted of tenants and squatters – into its participative urban planning approach.[17] That included policies that prioritized restoration over demolition, and that were geared towards protecting low-income populations from expulsion. In addition, residents who were affected by urban regeneration projects were to be consulted and involved in urban planning decisions by active participation where possible.[18] Furthermore, a programme for self-organized housing projects was implemented by the Senate of Berlin to help strengthen the personal involvement of tenants.[19]

Urban Pioneers

During the financial crisis in the first decade of the new millennium, investment for large project developments came to a halt. Very quickly, Berlin was transformed into an abandoned construction site thanks to a vast number of undeveloped locations and vacant buildings. The situation was exacerbated by Berlin's home-grown economic disaster, brought about by the collapse *Bankgesellschaft Berlin*. That particular crisis impelled the city to sell large swathes of land in order to counter the deficit in their financial administration. Plots and real estate were sold off cheaply, and oftentimes where investors did not yet want to develop.

---

17 Whereas the careful urban renewal approach of the 1980s executed in West Berlin was nearly 100% funded by the federal government (M. Bernt, B. Grell, and A. Holm, *The Berlin Reader: A Compendium on Urban Change and Activism* (Bielefeld: transcript, 2013), the financial support of this programme decreased substantially for its execution in the former part of East Berlin in the 1990s where 38 per cent was financed by government (H. Bodenschatz, C. Polinna, T. Govern and M. Huber, *Perspektiven einer IBA Berlin 2020: Ein strategisches Gutachten*. (Berlin: Senatsverwaltung für Stadtentwicklung, 2011)

18 Bernt *et al*, *The Berlin Reader*, op. cit. (note 17)

19 Policies like the Structural Self-Help (*Wohnungspolitische Selbsthilfe*) or the 'Muscle Mortgage' (*Muskelhypothek*) – essentially compensation for construction costs – (G. Jekel, *Vorstudie zur Einrichtung einer „Netzwerkagentur Generationenübergreifendes Wohnen"*, (Berlin: Senatsverwaltung für Stadtentwicklung, 2007) were introduced to contribute to individual and small-scale renovations in housing (Bodenschatz *et al*, *Perspektiven einer IBA Berlin 2020*, op. cit. (note 17)

At the same time, government funds for the preceding 'careful urban renewal programme' had come to an end. In the policies' place came a privately financed model that envisaged the transformation of rental places into private ownership. Part of this neoliberal strategy was the displacement of tenants, squashing the formerly established socially inclusive urban development goals that squatters and tenants had established.

In an emerging urbanism of austerity, proactive citizens came to the fore, to informally contribute to urban life in public spaces. So-called urban pioneers, they claimed vacant spaces to organize temporary events and set up cultural initiatives; a practice that has today become mainstream. In doing so, urban pioneers demonstrated to policy makers not only that vacant plots of land can better be used temporarily by the public, but that they can also improve the social interaction of communities, help tackle the need for communal places, and kickstart creativity. Making use of derelict warehouses and former industrial premises, they organized temporary, hands-on activities to revive desolate neighbourhoods with everything from climbing walls, flea markets, and concerts, to pop-up stores, skateparks and city farms. Urban pioneers called for policies that, 'seek to offer space to community (non-profit) projects.'[20]

Issuing a publication on the relevance and impact of urban pioneers on the liveability of the city itself, the Senator for Urban Development at the time, Ingeborg Junge-Reyer, denominated Berlin as a 'laboratory for the business of temporary use.'[21] Therefore, the municipality took up the task to find ways to mediate and coordinate the interests of property owners, temporary users and civil society. An often-voiced criticism towards the government was that its planners regarded these temporary activities solely as a means to an end, to raise the city's economic prospects – rather than as a serious strategy to include in future urban schemes.

Those Who Think the City Anew

When land prices started to rise drastically in inner-city areas in the second decade of this century, construction began to increase. With significantly less land lying undeveloped (or set aside for building), urban pioneers disappeared from urban development talks and plans. Instead, citizens looked for new ways

---

20 K. Overmeyer and H. Lauinger, *Urban Pioneers: Berlin: Stadtentwicklung durch Zwischennutzung*, (Berlin: Jovis, 2007) 24
21 Overmeyer and Lauinger, *Urban Pioneers*, op. cit. (note 20) 17

to engage in real-estate politics and governance. Together with governmental and private parties, they engaged more formally with the administration to advocate longer-term communal uses of vacant buildings. One such example is the Re-Thinking the City Initiative that was founded in 2011 as a cooperative model of civic participation in reaction to the sale and development of former market hall, Blumengroßmarkt. In 2012, citizens initiated a Round Table for Real Estate Politics – or *Runder Tisch Liegenschaftspolitik* – that aims to initiate a dialogue between the city government and civil society for transparent real estate politics.[22] One of their demands is a halt to the practice of selling publicly owned buildings and land for a maximum price. This politically independent platform continues to take place in the parliament building about four times per year. Together with deputies of different political parties, professional bodies, representatives of civil society, tenants' associations and city government, the aim of the Round Table is to develop policy tools that can be put in place to realign the city's real estate politics.

In parallel, and as a result of the earlier banking crisis and repeated critique of the mismanagement of state-owned properties, the Senate decided on a realignment of its real estate politics in 2010. This resulted in guidelines for a transparent real estate policy and a re-organization of institutional authorities.[23] In 2016, the government underscored in the coalition agreement to engage in more robust dialogue with civil society, and include participation into urban development plans. As a result, in Berlin it is not only the national government that can steer new development priorities, but overwhelmingly district offices that can exercise local power: they have the right to finalize local development plans within the framework of the city-wide Land Use Plan. Recent examples include Google's 2018 ditching of plans to build a headquarters in Berlin's Kreuzberg neighbourhood as a direct result of ongoing protests against gentrification in the area.

Likewise, the city's eventual and fiercely debated acquisition of the Dragoner Areal, also in Kreuzberg, which until 2017 was at risk of sale to the highest bidder.

---

22 *Runder Tisch Liegenschaftspolitik*, or *der Runde Tisch zur Neuausrichtung der Berliner Liegenschaftspolitik* has been debating issues of land politics in the Berlin House of Representatives since 2011. See https://stadtneudenken.net/runder-tisch/

23 The first steps of this transparent real estate policy were exemplified by the merging of the two federal real estate companies BIM and Liegenschaftsfonds Berlin (LFB) in 2015 through the Senate. I. Knop, Migration at record speed – the fusion of federal state real-estate companies in Berlin, *IT&I Magazine* (2016) no. 22. Available HTTP: https://www.openpromos.com/magazine22_article03/

The site has been rebranded 'Rathausblock': a German term that implies a mass of people around the city hall, or a place open to all. The proposed privatization had already led to the creation of citizen group *Stadt von Unten*, and is a positive example of city and district governments' willingness to engage in dialogue and cooperate with civil society and its initiatives. As a model project it followed up the activities around the contested site of the former state central administration for statistics of East Germany at Alexanderplatz. There, the initiative Haus der Statistik was formed by artist collectives, activist citizens, architects and foundations, all aspiring for affordable communal places in the city. Their campaign resulted in the repurposing of the derelict site into a community-oriented and cooperative neighbourhood development in 2015. Along with Dragoner Areal they now serve as showcase examples for a new mode of cooperation between civil society and administration.[24] They are illustrative of bottom-up initiated multi-stakeholder cooperations that are driven by the relentless professional drive of creatives and activist citizens who fight to have a say in the making of our everyday environment.[25] One of the successes at Haus der Statistik is that the Senate and the district council decided to continue with the integrative participation process and collaboration, and develop a 'city hall of the future' for 2031, together with the input of Berlin's citizens.

---

24 Dragonerareal and Haus der Statistik are part of fourteen (inner-city) contested urban sites that have been declared special places, *Besondere Orte*, to be developed as showcase examples within Berlin city's government. See Sozialdemokratische Partei Deutschlands (SPD), Die Linke, & Bündnis 90/ Die Grünen (2016) *Berlin gemeinsam gestalten. Solidarisch. Nachhaltig. Weltoffen. Koalitionsvereinbarung 2016-2021*, Berlin.

25 In order to have a stronger position in the multi-stakeholder development, the initiative Haus der Statistik set up a cooperative for urban development in 2016, the ZUsammenKUNFT Berlin eG (ZKB). https://zusammenkunft.berlin/

The Role of Citizens in Steering Neighbourhood Development

In recent years, citizen initiatives as well as the government have advocated for a more cooperative approach to urban development. Through realizing showcase projects, they have taken the lead to demonstrate both to the administration as well as society at large that a city can be built on common values. In that sense, the following case studies illustrate how civic engagement has grown despite a lack of shared vision with regard to a common urban future.

Blumengroßmarkt

The Blumengroßmarkt is regarded as a replicable model and reference project for the reform of real estate politics. When the sale and development of the area underwent a dialogue process between market forces and civil society, civic protests asked for urban strategies to preserve an urban mix of uses, users and inhabitants. The former market hall was developed into a mixed-used area offering not just apartments but also ateliers, neighbourhood meeting rooms, as well as offices for social agencies. As the first concept-based allocation in Berlin, the Blumengroßmarkt was part of a tendering procedure. But unlike the highest-bidding procedure, the decisive factors in this process included the valuation of bidders' use concept. Its public success was mainly achieved through the engagement, participation and collaboration of citizens, architects, the city government and real estate developers that opposed land use policies in place and subsequently worked on its reform. The location of the site of the former wholesale flower market is close to Berlin's 'new old centre,' the Gendarmenmarkt, as well as the former Wall. As such, it has been in the slipstream of urban developments in nearby districts for several decades. After the reunification in 1990 it became once again part of the largely prosperous inner-city area. The opening of the Jewish Museum in early 2000 had a major impact on the envisioned role of the area as a new creative place that would ensure social inclusion of the urban development to come.

Against this backdrop, various processes were started in order to define the main cornerstones for the future development of the site. In 2009, the district Friedrichshain-Kreuzberg initiated a study aimed at helping to define guidelines for project development for an inclusive artistic and creative neighbourhood. At its crux was establishing an internationally, as well as locally, well-connected district that would facilitate vibrant cultural and social interactions between future residents, cultural entrepreneurs and other stakeholders in the area. In 2010, the department for economy and urban development of the Friedrichshain-Kreuzberg district council started a marketing process for a concept-based sale in cooperation with public participation. To determine key objectives, award criteria and tools for urban development, a dialogue planning process was carried out by the planning office under the guidance of the district mayor in 2011. A rupture in the process occurred when the Berlin Real Estate Fund put the site on sale in 2011 without consulting all of the parties to the proceedings, and without incorporating the results of the dialogue planning meetings. The aim to facilitate a concept procedure that allows non-commercial prospective buyers to bid for the site was apparently abandoned and doors were opened again to unbridled market forces. In order to fight another sell-out to the highest-bidding investor, an initiative of citizens wrote an open letter to the city asking it to stop this procedure and stick to innovative and future-oriented land use policies instead.[26]

This civic protest turned into a broadly sustained participation within the realignment of the city's urban development policies. The successful initiative of the open letter not only helped to stop a sell-out of the Blumengroßmarkt, but was also the beginning of a long-term civic engagement in real-estate politics of the City of Berlin. The citizens involved founded the Re-Thinking The City Initiative to question rights and ownership of the city – ranging from large property investment projects to tenants' initiatives.

ExRotaprint

ExRotaprint is a 10,000-square-metre cluster of 1950s heritage buildings in Berlin's Wedding district. Once the site of a factory for Rotaprint printing presses, it now hosts artist studios, workspaces, creative industries of all kinds, community outreach organizations, event space, a neighbourhood canteen, and guest apartments. Its wide-ranging programme makes ExRotaprint a dynamic force in this multicultural north-western borough of the city. More significant still, the artist-launched initiative marked the first model of hereditary building lease in the German capital, with the explicit goal of safeguarding low rents and living security for the diverse local users and residents.

Effectively a form of shared tenure, a hereditary building lease separates ownership of land from ownership of its buildings, with the two parties entering into a

---

26 The open letter was written by participants of the conference *Kunst Stadt Berlin 2020* and was signed by 150 people engaged in the cultural and creative sector. See Kunst Stadt Berlin 2020 (2011) *Offener Brief: Liegenschaftspolitik in Berlin am Ende*, https://stadtneudenken.net/initiative/offener-brief/.

contract for a set duration of time. In the case of ExRotaprint, the land is owned by two nonprofit foundations – Stiftung Edith Maryon and Stiftung Trias – while the buildings are owned by ExRotaprint gGmbH, the driving force of which are artists Daniela Brahm and Les Schliesser.

Artists and entrepreneurs had long been present on the site: when the buildings' eponymous printing firm went bankrupt in 1989, the district rented the spaces for short-term use to creatives. However, when Berlin's banking crisis occurred in 2002, the district transferred ownership of the buildings to the Berlin Real Estate Fund – or *Liegenschaftsfonds* – the function of which was to sell city-owned land to the highest bidder. The community of artists already working from the site campaigned to save the buildings from demolition, and leave the land open and accessible for the neighbourhood.

With the setup of the tenants' association ExRotaprint e.V. in 2005, the initiators strengthened their political standing to pursue a commercially viable concept for acquiring the property. Brahm and Schliesser led negotiations with the District Council, the Senate and the Berlin Real Estate Fund to strike a deal to take over ownership of the buildings. During negotiations over a lease of the property with the Berlin Real Estate Fund, the association learned that the Fund had included the site in a wide-reaching portfolio package for hedge funds – a fact that it had failed to disclose to tenants. When an Icelandic investor expressed interest in buying the site in 2006 with the intention of transforming it into an attractive new housing development, it seemed inevitable that the Fund would sell.

Despite chances to purchase the site being slim, the tenants association kept fighting to develop the property from the bottom up. Activating political and social support against the sale, they built up a strong network within Berlin politics and civil society. With the backup of a financial analysis attesting the non-profitability of the derelict site due to high operational and heating costs, the initiative approached the Icelandic investor during a visit in 2007, requesting the ExRotaprint property be excluded from the portfolio. Concurrently, they intensified their public case, winning support from the Senate as well as the district to keep the site available for the neighbourhood and its community organizations.

With support from the foundations Edith Maryon and Trias – specifically their buying of the land – that same year, the newly established charitable company, ExRotaprint gGmbH was able to purchase the site's buildings for € 600,000 from the city of Berlin. As part of the 99-year-long hereditary leasehold entered into by both parties, ExRotaprint pays the foundations a ground rent of 10 per cent of net rental income, which amounts to €42,000 annually.[27] The partnership has not only secured the buildings as socially responsible places of residence and work, it has also maintained the independence of residents and entrepreneurs, all the while allowing for careful renovation of the historic site.

Although a first for Berlin, ExRotaprint, together with the foundations Trias and Edith Maryon, is representative of a growing number of organizations engaged in contributing to a non-capitalist market for real estate that serves the common good by helping to acquire land and properties to remove them from speculation. Others include the German Tenements Syndicate (a network of cohousing projects), philanthropic institutions, and other third sector parties. To make land use decisions transparent for Berlin citizens and initiate restructuring processes for urban development policies, ExRotaprint has elaborated on ownership models such as land lease constructions within a broader spectrum of diverse stakeholders and parties, aiming to broaden the scope of Berlin's land policy. Therefore, it has been actively involved in various civic initiatives of Berlin such as the previously mentioned Round Table for Real Estate Politics and the Re-Thinking the City Initiative. Since its implementation, the urban actors have continued to promote the model of building leases as a tool for stewardship in the development of socio-cultural places in Berlin.

27 When they have paid back the purchase price of the land, the annual ground rent will flow into the financing of new projects for the common good. https://www.exrotaprint.de/en/finanzieren/

Conclusion

Despite some of the good intentions of the city of Berlin with regard to integrative and responsible urban development, high demand for housing threatens to compromise its efforts. Further tension comes from the fact that participatory processes are time-consuming, potentially slowing the construction of much-needed new housing projects. Its city-building processes no longer mirror the literal construction site of 1990s Berlin; rather, the city is 'under construction,' and pitches itself as a social entity that is working on redefining itself. To that end, it aims to engage multiple stakeholders from government, private parties and civil society to safeguard 'a common good' – all the while keeping in check the strong pull from (financial) market forces. As part of this process, civilian-spearheaded initiatives have gained an ever-increasing influence on Berlin politics. Nevertheless, their success still depends on the political willingness of the city's administration.

In mapping the historical shifts of Berlin's planning culture and participative planning in particular, the role of 1980s squatting culture cannot be underestimated. From it emerged the top-down strategy of careful urban renewal which has contributed to a more empowered civil society. Indeed, the protests for small-scale urban development and affordable housing that squatters and housing activists fought for made significant impact on urban policies. Since then, Berlin's planning culture has moved fast as population growth forces authorities to rethink its precarious housing market that threatens to push out low-income groups. At the same time, Berlin has become an attractive investment option for developers, forcing authorities to balance the pressure to sell yet more land, with the needs of Berliners. This conflict has prompted the equally rapid maturing of participatory processes, particularly with regard to how civic initiatives are heard, and Berliners' perception of 'their' right to the city. Specifically, they have moved from angry protests in the 1980s and 1990s; to the creative vision of urban pioneers; to organized and politically influential civic initiatives ('those who think the city anew').

It is not just Berlin's planning and participatory processes that have evolved; its citizen actors have too. Many of those citizens active today have been so since the early 2000s. Concerned with economic independence and social equality, most began as independent volunteers, before becoming the cornerstones of more professional civilian organizations. It is a group of so-called citizen professionals and entrepreneurial citizens who have conquered a position in today's political landscape as urban professionals that policy makers and private market parties seem not to be able to neglect anymore. The implementation of discursive and critical platforms such as the Round Table for Real Estate Politics to test and discuss formats like the hereditary building lease or concept-based allocation further contributed to lay a base for future adaptations within Berlin's administrative policies for urban planning.

Civic initiatives have successfully shown that it is possible for bottom-up actions to influence urban development politics. As fieldwork on these cases has proven, Berlin citizens seem to be strongly convinced that they as civil society are 'entitled' to steer urban governance processes. And more importantly, the mindset of the city administration has started to change: it is not only citizen-led initiatives that engage for a just development of the city; certain district councils in Berlin make use of their political power as local planning authorities as well – as demonstrated by Haus der Statistik and Dragoner Areal, among others.

In Berlin, the relationship between government, private parties and civic initiatives have been constantly evolving and mutating. Realities and visions concerning urban development are thus continuously renegotiated. And although citizen initiatives might not always win initially – as illustrated at ExRotaprint – the long-term engagement, exchange, and struggle for adaptive urban policies cannot be underestimated. As these projects show, negotiations between government and civic initiatives continue to progress. However, the question of a just urban development for all remains an issue to be discussed. Or put another way, *forever to become and never to be.*

Bibliography

Arandjelovic, B. and Bogunovich, D., 'City Profile: Berlin', *Cities* (2014), 37

Bernt M., Grell B., and Holm A., *The Berlin Reader: A Compendium on Urban Change and Activism* (Bielefeld: transcript, 2013)

Bodenschatz, H., Polinna, C., Goevert, T., and Huber, M., *Perspektiven einer IBA Berlin 2020: Ein strategisches Gutachten* (Berlin: Senatsverwaltung für Stadtentwicklung, 2011)

Brahm, D., *Runder Tisch Liegenschaftspolitk: Erbbaurechte in Berlin: Dokumentation der ExpertenWERKSTATT* (Berlin: Initiative Stadt Neudenken and Stiftung trias , 2017)

Christof, K., 'The Citizen Professional, Mediatization, and the Creation of a Public Domain', Culture Unbound (2017) 9(3), 279–306

Deschermeier P., 'Bevölkerungsentwicklung in den deutschen Bundesländern bis 2035', *Institut der deutschen Wirtschaft Köln*, March 2018. Online. Available HTTP: https://www.iwkoeln.de/fileadmin/publikationen/2017/357919/IW-Trends_2017-03-04_Deschermeier.pdf

Garmer, M. 'Berlin endlich regierbar machen!' *Der Tagesspiegel* (21 February 2018). Online. Available HTTP: https://www.tagesspiegel.de/berlin/probleme-in-der-verwaltung-berlin-endlich-regierbar-machen/20984010.html.

Grimberg, K., 'Stadtplanung in Berlin "Was fehlt, ist eine Vision"' (18 April 2018). Online. Available HTTP: https://www.tagesspiegel.de/stadtplanung-in-berlin-was-fehlt-ist-eine-vision/21164672.html

Hou, J. (ed.) *Insurgent Public Space: Guerilla Urbanism and the Remaking of Contemporary Cities* (London and New York: Routledge, 2010)

Jekel, G.,*Vorstudie zur Einrichtung einer "Netzwerkagentur Generationenübergreifendes Wohnen"* (Berlin: Deutsches Institut für Urbanistik, Senatsverwaltung für Stadtentwicklung Berlin, 2007)

Krüger, A., 'Local Communities and Urban Regeneration: The Contribution of Community Education', *Community Development Journal* (1993) 28(4)

Lafond, M. A., 'eXperimentcity: Cultivating Sustainable Development in Berlin's Freiräume', in: J. Hou (ed.), *Insurgent Public Space: Guerilla Urbanism and The Remaking of Contemporary Cities* (London and New York: Routledge, 2010)

Löw, M. 'The City as Experiential Space: The Production of Shared Meaning', *International Journal of Urban and Regional Research* (2013) 37(3)

Ngo, A.-L., and Gordowy, O. (eds.) 'Berlin Theorie – Politik des Raums im Neuen Berlin', *ARCH+* (2021) *241*

Overmeyer, K., and Lauinger, H. (eds.) *Urban Pioneers: Berlin: Stadtentwicklung durch Zwischennutzung* (Berlin: Jovis, 2007)

Paffhausen, J., 'Bevölkerungsentwicklung Berlin', *Zeitschrift Für Amtliche Statistik Berlin/ Brandenburg* (2010) 3

Prantl, H., 'Berlin ohne Grund und Boden' *Blätter Für Deutsche Und Internationale Politik* (2017) 62(10). Online. Available HTTP: https://www.blaetter.de/archiv/jahrgaenge/2017/oktober/berlin-ohne-grund-und-boden

Scheffler, Karl, *Berlin, Ein Stadtschicksal* (1910) (Berlin: Fannei & Walz, 1989)

Schönball, R. and Zawatka-Gerlach, U. 'Rekommunalisierung in Berlin: Der Senat will Land für öffentliche Zwecke gewinnen', *Der Tagesspiegel* (8 January, 2018). Online. Available HTTP: https://www.tagesspiegel.de/berlin/rekommunalisierung-in-berlin-der-senat-will-land-fuer-oeffentliche-zwecke-gewinnen/20821244.html

Schulz, B., '15 Jahre "Arm, aber sexy" Spruch: Und heute? Reich, aber öde!', *Taz.de* (10 November 2018). Online. Available HTTP: http://www.taz.de/!5546816/

Senate Department for Urban Development and the Environment *et al. Berlin Strategy: Urban Development Concept Berlin 2030* (Berlin, 2015). Online. Available HTTP: www.stadtentwicklung.berlin.de/planen/stadtentwicklungskonzept/download/strategie/BerlinStrategie_Broschuere_en.pdf

Stahl, G., 'Cowboy Capitalism: The Art of Ping Pong Country in the New Berlin', *Space and Culture* (2008) 11

Vasudevan, A., *The Autonomous City: A History of Urban Squatting* (London and New York: Verso, 2017)

Senatsverwaltung für Stadtentwicklung und Umwelt Berlin (ed.) *Handbuch zur Partizipation* (Berlin: Kulturbuch-Verlag GmbH, 2011)

Wietschorke, J., 'So tickt Berlin? Städtische Eigenlogiken in der Diskussion', *Politik und Zeitgeschichte*/bpb.de (2017). Online. Available HTTP: http://www.bpb.de/apuz/260056/so-tickt-berlin-staedtische-eigenlogiken-in-der-diskussion

Wowereit, K. and Lauer, E., *Sexy, aber nicht mehr so arm: mein Berlin* (Berlin: Edel Books, (2018)

Zimmer, E. and Schoenecker, K., 'Entwicklung der Grundstücksverkäufe in Berlin und Brandenburg', *Zeitschrift Für Amtliche Statistik* (2019) 4

HAMBURG

BRÜCKE 3
HAFENTERRASSE
HOCHBAHN

How Bürger and Dissent Logics Shape Participatory Processes

Identifying and Tracing Intrinsic Logics in Hamburg Urban Development Projects

Michiel Stapper, Cathrin Zengerling and Renée Tribble

In this chapter we investigate how intrinsic logics of Hamburg shape participatory processes. Set against the backdrop of Hamburg's oftentimes contentious history – be that social, political, or spatial – at its crux is the shifting relationship between commercial parties, government agencies and residents. We present an overview of the history of Hamburg and two specific historical repertoires. Next, we show how these historical repertoires act as intrinsic logics in contemporary urban development in Hamburg. An ongoing exchange, the resultant tensions are witnessed in several recent urban development projects, two of which will be scrutinized in greater detail. We use the development projects of Neue Mitte Altona and Paloma Viertel, the so-called Esso-Häuser, as exemplary cases since they give insight into how intrinsic logics can clash and complement each other.

While participation is often organized, the amount of influence that citizens can have varies greatly from project to project. Moreover, there seems to be a participation paradox: increased participation has not led to increased influence.[1] In this chapter we investigate how intrinsic logics can help us understand how participatory processes are perceived and valued. Participatory processes will need different characteristics in different neighbourhoods in order to be seen as legitimate by neighbourhood residents.

Our approach to identifying and tracing intrinsic logics in Hamburg's urban development is threefold. Firstly, we delineate two central logics from an analysis of patterns in the historical repertoire of the city. Secondly, we link the identified logics to urban development processes and scrutinize if and how they are reproduced in current urban development structures, processes and instruments. We are aware that there are more intrinsic logics active in Hamburg, but these two are consistently reproduced through time. It is important to us to find out if there is an interplay between the intrinsic logics and the administrative system and its practice. Thirdly, we aim to trace the intrinsic logics in two specific case studies: Esso-Häuser and Neue Mitte Altona. We have conducted 21 interviews with key actors in Hamburg and one of the authors of this chapter was an active participant in the Esso-Häuser case.

Hamburg's Historical Repertoire: Two Intrinsic Logics

We argue that throughout the history of Hamburg two intrinsic logics have been reproduced decade after decade. We start our analysis with the legends of how Hamburg was founded and end with World War Two. The first logic can be defined as the Bürger logic, which stands for economic independence; uses legal instruments to order the social; values commercial successful people like merchants and traders; and justifies pragmatic politics. This is connected to Hamburg's self-image of depending on a flourishing harbour for a prosperous city,[2] and is also reflected in being a member of the Hanse. Bürger were urban, privileged citizens, often merchants, that governed the city. Regarded as decent, civil and honest citizens, they formed a historical social class in between the nobility, the

---

1 J.R. Levine, 'The paradox of community power: cultural processes and elite authority in participatory governance', *Social Forces* (2017) 95(3), 1155–1179

2 M. Rodenstein, 'Die Eigenart der Städte – Frankfurt und Hamburg im Vergleich', in: M. Löw and H. Berking, *Die Eigenlogik der Städte* (Frankfurt and New York: Campus, 2008) 261-311

clergy and peasants. Although the tier of Bürger does not exist anymore, their moral qualities and logics are still valued today. The second logic is the dissent logic, which relates to those that are excluded from the benefits and protection of the law and privileges of the Bürger; uses activism to order the social; values outlaws, marginalized people and non-conformists; and revolves around the politics of emancipation and empowerment (*Selbst-Ermächtigung*).

The Bürger logic is illustrated in the legends surrounding how Hamburg achieved its city rights – such as autonomy in specific areas of law and trading rights – in the Middle Ages, although the exact dates of this are disputed. It is believed that Hamburg was granted free trading rights by Emperor Barbarossa in 1189 and was thereafter known as the Free Imperial City of Hamburg.[3] However, there are others who claim that these city rights were made up by Hamburg merchants in 1225.[4] Either way, both stories show how traders and merchants strived for independence, which is in line with the Bürger logic. Another medieval story – also with murky credibility – illustrates how ingrained this Bürger logic is in Hamburg's history. The legend centres on Hein Brandt, a Bürger in medieval Hamburg, who had lent a large sum of money to the Duke of Sachsen-Lauenburg. Although Brandt sent multiple requests to be paid back the money, the Duke ignored him. When the Bürger Brandt saw the Duke in Hamburg, he confronted him and demanded to be repaid. The Duke replied that because he had the protection of the city council, Brandt could not force him to do anything. Brandt understandably became angry and started to shout at the Duke, prompting the aristocrat to complain to the council about the Bürger's improper behaviour. The city council immediately summoned Hein Brandt, questioned him and sent him to prison. The decision provoked anger among the people of Hamburg: just five years prior, the council had adopted an act that every citizen had the right to a fair and honest trial. In the eyes of the people, the injustice against Brandt was far from an isolated incident, and so the citizens of Hamburg took to the streets. Fearful of the rebellious crowds, the city council of Hamburg adopted its first constitution.[5] The document included a law stating that anyone who still owed money to citizens of Hamburg was barred from entering the city. Hein Brandt was duly released, and his story became emblematic of the city, and in particular,

---

3 D. Rodnick, *A Portrait of Two German Cities: Lübeck and Hamburg* (Lubbock, Texas: The Caprock Press, 1980)

4 E. Verg and M. Verg, *Das Abenteuer das Hamburg heißt* (4th ed.), (Hamburg: Ellert&Richter, 2007)

5 Verg and Verg, *Das Abenteuer das Hamburg*, op. cit. (note 4)

Bürger logic. Indeed, still today a street in Hamburg bears his name: Brandstwiete. Although the particularities – who are the involved actors, what are the specific political debates – change over time, the pull towards political independence and economic prosperity is strong in Hamburg.

Hamburg's dissent logic is embodied by the stretch of land between its city walls and the historic city of Altona, which was independent until 1937 and is now a neighbourhood of Hamburg. Now the site of two streets – Große Freiheit and Kleine Freiheit – also known simply as Freiheit (Freedom Area), it was once an intermediate space whose residents were excluded from the benefits and protection of the law.[6] The former city of Altona had its origins in a trading centre on the River Elbe, launched by Danish and Swedish kings who envied Hamburg's wealth. During the Reformation, Hamburg embraced Lutheranism and rejected other religions. Thus, Altona became a safe haven for religious refugees and Jews during the wars of the sixteenth century. In this area, all kinds of activities were allowed – as long as the citizens of Hamburg were not affected negatively.[7] At the time, it was a place where artisans could sell goods duty-free and brothels could operate. Centuries later, the area has evolved into a neighbourhood that is known for its left-wing politics and activism.

Both the Bürger and dissent logics have been reproduced through Hamburg's history. For example, after the religious wars of the sixteenth and seventeenth centuries, the eighteenth century welcomed an era of much economic growth in Hamburg.[8] In this period, the Bürgers took pride in their economic prosperity and long independent tradition. Money earned by merchants was partly invested in public service projects, for example. And despite the fact that only citizens who owned property and paid taxes had voting rights, the majority of Hamburg's inhabitants took pride in its independence.[9] This illustrates that the Bürger logic was not only valued by the Bürger themselves, but other social classes too. Its success was reproduced and promoted by Hamburg's influential newspaper and publishing industry, and the city's media sector would go on to become Europe's second-largest after London.[10]

---

6 Rodnick, *A Portrait of Two German Cities*, op. cit. (note 3)
7 Rodnick, *A Portrait of Two German Cities*, op. cit. (note 3)
8 M. Lindemann, *The merchant republics: Amsterdam, Antwerp, and Hamburg, 1648–1790* (New York: Cambridge University Press, 2015)
9 K.B. Aaslestad, *Place and Politics: local identity, civic culture, and German nationalism in North Germany during the Revolutionary era* (Leiden and Boston: Brill Academic Publishers, 2005)
10 Aaslestad, *Place and Politics*, op. cit. (note 9)

As the logics adapted to new circumstances, their core purpose remained the same, but the specific meanings attached to them underwent changes. To illustrate, the Napoleonic Wars of 1803 to 1815 brought the occupation of Hamburg by the French and the dissolution of the Holy Roman Empire.[11] After the liberation of the city from the French, Hamburg became a sovereign state within the German Confederation. When Hamburg was included in the North German Confederation and later in the German Empire it was able to maintain its independence. Hamburg prospered within the German Empire, and became the second-largest harbour of Europe. Its success attracted labourers from outside the city, and soon, heavy manufacturing moved to the suburbs – close to the 'Freedom Area' – due to overcrowding of the inner centre. This period increasingly saw clashes between dissent and Bürger logics: the privileges of the Bürger class were challenged by socialist-leaning labourers, who justified their actions – such as strikes and demonstrations – using the dissent logic. The labourers became a strong force in Hamburg politics. When the Social Democratic Party was dissolved by Chancellor Bismarck in 1878, his rule was not enforced by the Hamburg senate.[12] The Bürger logic was invoked to portray the socialist labourers as foreigners, appropriating the rights of the Bürgers.[13] They were especially accused of lacking *bürgerliche* honesty and being incapable of defending the freedoms of Hamburg.[14] This shows that although Hamburg rejected Bismarck's prohibition of the Social Democratic Party, the Bürger logic was used to suppress the socialist party and its allies.

Interestingly, the Socialists in Hamburg have always been less radical than those in other parts of Germany. The most radical socialist party, the Independent Socialists, never attracted much support.[15] During the revolts in the aftermath of World War One – the November Revolution – Hamburg saw significantly less uprising among workers than other German cities; its workers were more concerned with improving their own living conditions, rather than overthrowing the government.[16] In the then-city of Altona, however, mass strikes and socialist demonstrations were commonplace. Later on, the city lost its privileges concerning legislation during the Nazi regime, resulting in revolt. On 17 July 1932, the

---

11 Rodnick, *A Portrait of Two German Cities*, op. cit. (note 3)
12 Rodnick, *A Portrait of Two German Cities* op. cit. (note 3)
13 M. Hurd, *Public Spheres, Public Mores, and Democracy Hamburg and Stockholm 1870-1914* (Ann Arbor: The University of Michigan Press, 2000)
14 Hurd, *Public Spheres*, op. cit. (note 13)
15 Rodnick, *A Portrait of Two German Cities*, op. cit. (note 3)
16 Rodnick, *A Portrait of Two German Cities*, op. cit. (note 3)

rebellion was crushed by the Nazis on a day of bloodshed and massacre: Altonian Bloody Sunday. The leaders of the demonstration were arrested and beheaded a year later.[17]

Hamburg was also not spared from Nazi crimes: as the city with the greatest Jewish population of Germany at that time, a majority of this population did not survive the Nazi regime. Many of the Socialist and Communist leaders of Hamburg were also transported to concentration camps. Furthermore, as an important industrial centre, the city was severely bombed during World War Two.

Bürger and Dissent Logics in Contemporary Urban Development

After World War Two, Hamburg regained its special status as the Free and Hanseatic City of Hamburg in the Federal Republic of Germany. Years later, its economy benefited greatly from the reunification of Germany in 1990. Hamburg fast became the media capital of Germany, and its harbour fuelled economic prosperity.[18]

For more than 60 of the approximately 75 years since the end of World War Two, Hamburg has been governed by the Social Democrat Party (SDP), including more than four consecutive decades (1957 until 2001) with one of its politicians as mayor. Among Europe's wealthiest cities during the 1960s, the economic crisis beginning in the 1970s entailed a strong focus on regaining economic prosperity, also via urban development. During the 1980s the Social Democrat mayors Dohanyi and Voscherau coined the term "Enterprise Hamburg" ('*Unternehmen Hamburg*') as the urban development vision for the years to come.[19] It encompassed the strengthening of several industrial and business sectors as well as an

---

17 C. Zentner and F. Bedürftig, *The encyclopedia of the third reich* (New York: Macmillan, 1991)
18 J. Friedrich, 'Social inequality, segregation and urban conflict: the case of Hamburg', in: S. Musterd and W. Ostendorf (eds.) *Urban Segregation and the Welfare State: Inequality and exclusion in western cities* (London and New York: Routledge, 1998), 191–206
19 Klaus von Dohnanyi, 'Unternehmen Hamburg', speech at Hamburg Übersee-Club on 29 November 1983, available at: http://www.ueberseeclub.de/resources/Server/pdf-Dateien/1980-1984/vortrag-1983-11-29Dr.%20Klaus%20von%20Dohnanyi.pdf

"economization of the administration."[20] The later vision on urban development, 'Metropole Hamburg – Wachsende Stadt' (translated as 'Metropolis Hamburg – Growing City'), established by the Christian Democratic (CDU) mayor Ole von Beust;[21] and on a project level, the urban development project of HafenCity can be seen in the light of this spirit.[22] The economy- and growth-focused visions for Hamburg urban development, essentially shared by Social and Christian Democrat mayors throughout the last four decades, can be interpreted as driven by an underlying Bürger logic, inherent – in different facets – in the political agendas of both centre-leaning parties.

Among the most visible traces of the dissent logics is the *Recht auf Stadt* – or 'right to the city' – movement, rooted in the protest against Ole von Beust's CDU government of Hamburg from 2001 to 2010.[23] In retaliation against perceived gentrification promoted by urban policies based on the 'Growing City' vision, which was aimed at boosting economic competitiveness and 'upgrading' various quarters of the city,[24] the Recht auf Stadt movement mobilized thousands of Hamburgers to join demonstrations. In another prominent act of dissent, in August 2009 artists and activists occupied the Gängeviertel, a large historic building complex in the centre of Hamburg, to save it from demolition and turn it into a space for arts, culture and debates.[25] Further prominent bottom-up urban development initiatives driven by Recht auf Stadt dissent logics are Park Fiction,[26] Viktoria Kaserne,[27] and the Esso-Häuser. Dissent logics are also inherent in regular demonstrations. They include the annual 1 May demos, which are centered in the alternative quarter of Schanzenviertel; and famously in 2017, when the SPD led the city, large protests against the G20 meeting which was being held in Hamburg. With

---

20 P. Birke, 'Herrscht hier Banko? Die aktuellen Proteste gegen das Unternehmen Hamburg', *Sozial. Geschichte Online* (2010), 3, 148-191, 155

21 O. Von Beust, 'Das Leitbild:"Metropole Hamburg—Wachsende Stadt,"' in: *Wachsende Stadt* (Hamburg: VS Verlag für Sozialwissenschaften, 2004)

22 P. Birke, 'Herrscht hier Banko?', op. cit. (note 20). For a detailed analysis highlighting strengths and weaknesses of the HafenCity development see T. Krüger, 'HafenCity Hamburg–ein Modell für moderne Stadtentwicklung', *RaumPlanung* (2009) (146), 193-198. More critical is J. Menzel, 'Wie nachhaltig ist die HafenCity Hamburg' (Hamburg: Zukunftsrat Hamburg, 2010)

23 J. Novy and C. Colomb, 'Struggling for the right to the (creative) city in Berlin and Hamburg: New urban social movements, new "spaces of hope"?', *International Journal of Urban and Regional Research* (2013) 37(5), 1816–1838;

24 Freie und Hansestadt Hamburg, *Räumliches Leitbild Entwurf: Wachsende Stadt - Grüne Metropole am Wasser*, (2007) Hamburg.

25 Birke, 'Herrscht hier Banko?' op. cit. (note 20) See also https://das-gaengeviertel.info/en.html

26 https://park-fiction.net/

27 https://www.fux-eg.org/

a view to the overall political landscape dissent logics may also partly justify why Hamburg is one of the few West German states in which the left-wing party, Die Linke, has been a member of the state parliament since 2008.

The dichotomy of Bürger and dissent logics is also apparent in structures and practices of the Hamburg administration. On the one hand, for example, the influence of consultancies on urban development strategies under the 'Growing City' paradigm is an expression of market oriented policies.[28] Further examples include the roll out of several Business Improvement Districts (BIDs) based on a 2005 state law,[29] making Hamburg the first city in Germany to incorporate them. In addition is a long list of arguably top-down projects following the 'Growing City' paradigm.[30] On the other hand, it is important to note that Hamburg politicians and administration were open to negotiate 'compromises' with several initiatives of the Recht auf Stadt movement. They include projects like Park Fiction, Gängeviertel, Esso-Häuser and Viktoria Kaserne.

Several elements of the current administrative system and practice can be seen as an achievement of dissent logics entering the 'Enterprise Hamburg': In 2011, the Stadtwerkstatt Hamburg (agency to promote participation) was established by the Hamburg senate in response to a request from the state parliament.[31] Its goal was to establish a new planning culture which offers high quality participatory processes beyond the legally required minimum. Participation is partly outsourced to consultancy firms, to support the implementation of various forms of citizen participation. A newer development in this context is the establishment of DIPAS, or digital participation systems.[32] Last but not least, the most recent vision for Hamburg urban development published in 2014 is termed 'Green, Just

---

28 A. Vogelpohl, 'McKinseyisierung oder Regierungsprojekt? Unternehmensberatungen in der strategischen Stadtentwicklung. Das Beispiel "Metropole Hamburg–Wachsende Stadt"', *Raumforschung und Raumordnung-Spatial Research and Planning* (2017), 75(4), 327-338. For a fundamental review of these effects see J. Bogumil, S. Grohs, and S. Kuhlmann, 'Ergebnisse und Wirkungen kommunaler Verwaltungsmodernisierung in Deutschland–Eine Evaluation nach zehn Jahren Praxiserfahrung', *Politische Vierteljahreszeitschrift, Sonderheft* (2006) 37, 151-184

29 For a list of BIDs in Hamburg and their legal backbone see https://www.hamburg.de/bid-projekte/.

30 Freie und Hansestadt Hamburg, Behörde für Stadtentwicklung und Wohnen, 2019, Hamburger Projekte der Stadtentwicklung 2015-2030, See also project descriptions at https://www.hamburg.de/stadtplanung/projekte/.

31 Bürgerschaftsdrucksache 20/278. See also organizational structure of the department of urban development and housing at https://www.hamburg.de/bsw/.

32 https://www.hamburg.de/dipas/.

and Growing City on the Waterfront – Perspectives on Urban Development in Hamburg.' With a focus on justice, sustainability and growth, it can be interpreted as an infiltration of the Recht auf Stadt agenda into the former 'growth first' paradigm of the city.

Tracing Intrinsic Logics in Participatory Processes: The Cases of Esso-Häuser and Neue Mitte Altona

Bürger logic and the dissent logic are invoked in two development projects in Hamburg. One is the Esso-Häuser, which saw a group of planners, architects, social workers and artists come together to create a platform for the residents of Hamburg's legendary Reeperbahn area to influence local development. Elsewhere, Hamburg's second-largest development project to date – Neue Mitte Altona – put Germany's complex planning laws to the test. Both illustrative of Hamburg's unique citizen participation trajectories, the case studies are also emblematic of Hamburg's long-held reputation as an 'activist city.' Contrasting both cases shows how the intrinsic logics are adapted to organize collective action in contemporary Hamburg urban development. Furthermore, they show that logics can clash, but also supplement each other.

Esso-Häuser

The Reeperbahn is an infamous street in St. Pauli, Hamburg. It was Hamburg's poorest neighbourhood in 1989,[33] and used to be a home of the working class: harbour workers, migrants, and outsiders such as sex workers and transgender people. Fast-forward to today, however, and St. Pauli is getting more and more attractive to mid- and high-income groups, and is facing severe gentrification. It is located in the space between the city center of Hamburg and the former independent city of Altona, which was known as 'Freedom Area' (Freiheit). The area still embodies dissent logic and is a place for free minds and activities. Dubbed *Die sündigste Meile der Welt* – or most sinful mile of the world – the Reeperbahn is home to many bars, clubs and theatres. Although by day the Reeperbahn may seem lacking in colour, by night the street comes alive: neon lights promote sex

33 H. Manos, *Sankt Pauli : soziale Lagen und soziale Fragen im Stadtteil Sankt Pauli* (Hamburg: Ergebnisse, 1989)

shops' wares; and brothels and strip clubs open for business, including Europe's oldest S&M club, Club de Sade.

The street is also home to Esso-Häuser. Built in the aftermath of World War Two, the housing complex contained social housing, a hotel, clubs, a garage and a gas station (hence the name Esso-Häuser). Because it also sold groceries and was open 24/7, the gas station was a meeting point and melting pot of the area.

The Esso-Häuser was bought by the investor Bayerische Hausbau in 2009. With the intention of demolishing the buildings and developing a new complex, the owners asked tenants to sign new contracts. Claiming the originals were out-of-date, the replacement contracts proposed by Bayerische Hausbau significantly reduced tenants' rights. Specifically, they no longer guaranteed tenants could keep living in the housing complex, thereby making the path to demolition easier for Bayerische Hausbau.

On learning of the investor's demands at a tenants' meeting, neighbourhood organization GWA stepped in. A community organization for the St. Pauli district, GWA's scope includes cultural projects, social work and health, and campaigning for affordable housing. Employees went door to door in the Esso-Häuser to inform tenants of their rights and warn them to not sign the new contract. The Esso-Häuser Initiative was established to unite tenants, neighbours and business owners, and with the aim of preventing demolition of the complex and protecting the rights of tenants. Their actions soon caught the attention of the media, making the proposed demolition of the Esso-Häuser a widely discussed topic in Hamburg and a symbol of gentrification. The community organization invoked the dissent logic, claiming the need to protect the counter culture in St. Pauli.

In order to decrease tensions in the area, in 2011 the Bayerische Hausbau started roundtable talks with the Esso-Häuser Initiative about the future of the complex. However, the meetings failed to improve relations and in 2012, Bayerische Hausbau ended the dialogue due to a perceived unwillingness to compromise on the part of Esso-Häuser Initiative. By ending the roundtables, Bayerische Hausbau created an obstacle in getting plans approved, and were warned by alderman Andy Grote that plans needed approval by the district.[34] In reaction, the Esso-Häuser Initiative issued a manifesto, supported by some of Hamburg's

---

34 L. Kaiser, 'Kein Abriss ohne Kompromiss', *Die Tageszeitung*, 9 February 2012

most prominent public figures. The manifesto demanded that the Esso-Häuser complex be saved from demolition.[35] It also called for politics based on the needs of the people living in the St. Pauli neighbourhood, not politics in the name of the real estate industry. Again, the dissent logic is activated to organize collective action. By invoking the dissent logic the authors of the manifesto attempted to mobilize support from other actors critical of the urban development strategies of the municipality of Hamburg. Meanwhile, the Bayerische Hausbau warned that the building was at risk of collapse and positioned structural supports around the buildings.

In December 2013, the Esso-Häuser were evacuated by police. After reports of shaking walls and cars parked below being covered in dust, the *Bezirksamt* (district alderman) decided that it was not safe anymore to live in the building. The Esso-Häuser was thus demolished, and the goal of neighbourhood activists to maintain the building failed. This was a clear turning point in the story of the Esso-Häuser: although the building was razed, the people of St. Pauli still wanted to influence future plans. In an independent neighbourhood assembly they started to organize a democratic planning process.[36] To that end, a group of citizens comprising planners, architects, social workers and artists came together to form the group, PlanBude, with the intention of organizing the participation process. Because the demolition of the Esso-Häuser was very unpopular, there was a lot of pressure on Bayerische Hausbau and the *Bezirksamt* to agree to PlanBude's proposal. The municipality duly arranged funding and commissioned the PlanBude to organize the participative process. Thus, an organization that was more prone to representing the dissent logic found itself in charge of the participatory process of the Esso-Häuser.

The goal of PlanBude was to plan the new Esso-Häuser in a creative, bottom-up way whereby all citizens of St.Pauli could get involved – thereby activating Hamburg's dissent logic to reach their goal. Therefore they organized a six-month participatory process incorporating many creative planning methods and concepts. Its epicentre was a container that was put next to the building site, where people could visit, talk through their proposals, or give input on the plans. On its rooftop was a platform overlooking the site, and inside a small library encouraged local citizens to read about urban design. Visitors were also invited to use Lego

---

35 U. Gassdorf and M. Fischer, 'Prominente Abrissgegner', *Die Welt*, 2013
36 https://www.st-pauli-selber-machen.de/ballsaal-resolution/

or plasticine to express their ideas, or else draw them. Because the area around the Reeperbahn is infamous for its nightlife, PlanBude asked residents as well as passing tourists to think about how they wanted their neighbourhood to feel after dark, organized sound walks, and held a photo workshop. In addition to a survey to help quantify residents' input, there were seminars, readings, and even an urban education programme for the local school.

The input of the citizens was collected and presented in two community meetings. The first outlined tendencies in the outcomes of the participation process. In a second meeting, wishes and ideas were clustered to determine what would be important for the new development of the Esso-Häuser. Hereby, demands of the neighbourhood for the urban design, societal impact and functions were made visible. The results also formed the basis for the St. Pauli code, which comprises seven rules for local development.

1. Difference and Diversity before Homogeneity
2. Small Scale Structures
3. Low-Budget before Luxury (Cheap before Expensive)
4. Originality and Tolerance
5. Appropriation and Vibrancy
6. Experiment and Sub-Culture
7. Open Space Without Consumerism.[37]

The rules embody the dissent logic by placing the protection of subcultures and space for tolerance and non-conformists at the heart of the code. Moreover, the rules call for distinctiveness and the embracing of the 'trashy glamour' (*schmuddeliger Glamour*) of the neighbourhood. The St. Pauli code was used as a starting point for the design process. For the design competition, several architects were invited to visit the area. As well as being taken on guided tours of the district, the architects were also briefed on the results of the participation process. In turn, the neighbourhood provided feedback on proposals to help hone their designs. The final jury included two residents from St. Pauli, and ended up selecting a plan by Dutch architect Kamiel Klaasse. The design included roof tops with a basketball court and climbing wall; shops that matched St. Pauli's profile (including a queer-feminist sex shop); housing cooperatives (where ownership of the buildings

---

37 Planbude 'St. Pauli Code', (2015). Online. Available HTTP: https://planbude.de/st-pauli-code/ (accessed 11 June 2020)

are collectively owned, or *Baugemeinschaft* in German); social and market-rate housing; and a hotel. The market-rate housing and hotel were a compromise with the Bayerische Hausbau and the district representatives.

Although all parties were happy with the design, the negotiations about the final agreement were contentious due to a clash between dissent and Bürger logic. Involving the municipality, PlanBude and the Bayerische Hausbau, negotiations centered on specifying the building programme for the development. The prices of the housing cooperatives were an especially big issue. The Bayerische Hausbau wanted market rate prices for the housing cooperatives, while PlanBude demanded affordable prices. The negotiations were carried out under the supervision of an independent mediator which helped structure and organize them. However, once the budget for the mediator was exhausted, progress slowed significantly. Several times during the process, PlanBude indicated it was ready to walk away because the Bayerische Hausbau refused to compromise. Fortunately, however, in November 2018, the agreement was signed.

The neighbourhood of St. Pauli, and especially the Reeperbahn, have a unique history that shaped the development of the Esso-Häuser. Related, Hamburg's dissent logic is strongly connected to the district. It was formerly an area where activities prohibited within Hamburg's city walls could take place, and although most are now widely sanctioned, they are arguably extra visible on the streets of St. Pauli. The neighbourhood's code reproduces this dissent logic by placing emphasis on protecting subcultures, what it calls dirty glamour, and embracing everything that is outside the norm. The PlanBude team itself is also representative of this logic and the history of the area by virtue of being a transdisciplinary team of individuals with a strong connection to the neighbourhood, rather than expected planners and consultants. The fact that the Bayerische Hausbau is not from Hamburg but from South Germany also played a role. The neighbourhood is proud of symbols such as the St. Pauli football club, Astra beer and its working class reputation, so when wealthy investors from Bayern arrived on the scene, it triggered independence and resistance from the local community. Contrary to claims made by Bayerische Hausbau, the neighbourhood and PlanBude did compromise: the project contains market-rate housing and a hotel which fuels gentrification of the area. As such, Hamburg activism's more pragmatic inclination that is traceable through history is also visible.

Neue Mitte Altona

Founded by the Danish and located on the site of an eponymous former city that became home to Hamburg's religious outcasts, Altona is Hamburg's western-most district. It is the location of the Neue Mitte Altona project, which aims to build 2,500 housing units, public facilities and business space. The project is aimed for completion by around 2025. The second-largest development project of Hamburg, it is a result of German railway company Deutsche Bahn moving its station from Altona to Diebsteich, thereby creating space to develop housing. However, not all the property was owned by Deutsche Bahn; two large property owners and several smaller ones also owned land in the area. In order to develop the land, the municipality had to use a special planning instrument, *städtebauliche Entwicklungsmaßnahme* (urban development measure, section 165 of the German building code) to force the owners into an agreement. Under German planning law, this can only happen under very specific conditions. Specifically, the municipality must prove that the development is of critical importance to the general public. In most cases this is not possible, so the municipality must instead develop a well-grounded proposal. Deployment of this planning instrument presents land owners with the choice to either sell the land to the municipality at its current value, or come to an agreement. Because development frequently means a higher profit, the landowners often choose to negotiate an agreement. This is what happened in the Neue Mitte Altona project.

The municipality was adamant that negotiations took place before the public was involved, stating that this was a requirement of the planning tool. However, in public discourse the dissent logic was activated by arguing that the municipality was catering to real estate investors. The critique was in line with that of the Recht-auf-Stadt movement on urban politics in Hamburg. Due to strong criticism, the municipality found itself needing to balance the Bürger logic and the dissent logic. The city planners reached out to citizens that wanted to be involved in the development process and invited them to be part of a special group called the *Koordinierungsgremium*. This unit would negotiate with the municipality about the urban design and programme of Neue Mitte Altona. Because the *Koordinierungsgremium* aimed to be democratic and incorporate the interests of all residents, they organized assemblies in which they discussed the plans.

When the *Koordinierungsgremium* was established, they expected their decisions to be incorporated into the development plans. They reasoned that they provided the Neue Mitte Altona with necessary democratic legitimacy. However, the city planners had already made some agreements with landowners and had also their own policy goals. Therefore the municipality proposed an agreement that used the input of the *Koordinierungsgremium*, but did not incorporate all their demands. This was heavily criticized, invoking the dissent-logic. The agreement to set the land value relatively high was particularly controversial, since it would mean a high profit for the land owners. However, the municipality argued that the land value was set as part of the legally bound process of negotiations, and to force land owners into an agreement. Thus, the municipality used the Bürger logic to justify their actions. Ultimately, the *Koordinierungsgremium* felt that they were not taken seriously and collectively quit.[38] In a public statement they placed the Neue Mitte Altona project in a historic context, where market interests suppressed the interests of the residents of Altona. In doing so, they invoked the dissent logic to criticize the Bürger logic of the municipality of Hamburg.

Their resignation undermined the legitimacy of the Neue Mitte Altona plans. Nonetheless, the municipality pushed forward with the negotiations with landowners and the design of the plan. Because the municipality was responsible for the public infrastructure of Neue Mitte Altona, they could design the public park with the help of the neighbourhood residents. To that end, they organized focus groups with people that do not normally attend public meetings – such as people with a migration background – to gather input for its design. In addition, two citizens selected via a lottery could join the jury of the park's design competition. Because a majority of the jury opted to support whichever design was preferred by residents, the winning scheme ended up being that selected by these citizens.

Another important group of people that were involved in the Neue Mitte Altona were people with disabilities. This group of people was represented by the organization Q8. A foundation that empowers people to engage with urban policy, Q8 arranged a public meeting to gather ideas and input about how Neue Mitte Altona could become barrier-free for its disabled users. Under the banner of '*Eine Mitte für Alle*' – or, 'One Mitte District for All' – they made no fewer than 30 suggestions.[39] These ideas were formulated in such a way that they could easily be incorporated into contractual agreements, adhering to the Bürger logic. The list was presented to city planners, the *Bezirksamt* and members of the senate. Collectively, these agencies decided to incorporate the ideas generated by Q8 into the

---

38 Koordinierungsgremium Mitte Altona, 'Ein Moratorium für Mitte Altona', (2012)
39 Q8 'Konkretisierung inklusiver Strukturen in Mitte Altona: Empfehlungen des Forums Eine Mitte für Alle', (2015)

contractual agreement of not just Neue Mitte Altona, but all other development projects in Altona. The *Eine Mitte für Alle* process and plan was recognized and awarded by the UN as one of the best housing innovations of 2015. Interestingly, the residents that acted according to the Bürger logic were thus better able to direct Neue Mitte Altona towards their goals.

The final development contract of the Neue Mitte Altona project featured several elements that were included because of the participation processes.[40] The municipality was able to do this because they pressured the landowners to not further escalate conflict with the Recht auf Stadt movement. For example, during the negotiation process, the municipality took the land owners to assemblies and meetings with the *Koordinierungsgremium* to show how the project was perceived by the public. This helped with the implementation of public goals in the contractual agreements, such as community organizing, affordable rents for small-scale socially responsible businesses, and a barrier-free plan. However, the members of the *Koordinierungsgremium* argued that their ideas were watered down and essentially co-opted.

The Neue Mitte Altona project shows the Bürger logic of Hamburg's government agencies. According to the municipality the project was only possible by forcing the land owners into an agreement. However, this meant that public involvement in the project was not possible at the beginning of the process. Thus, the development of the project was more important than public outreach and debate. When the legitimacy of the project was severely undermined by the dissolution of the *Koordinierungsgremium*, the planners managed to recover the situation by organizing focus groups and including two citizens in the procurement process of the public land. They worked closely with Q8 to make the project barrier-free, and used the fierce criticism of the Recht auf Stadt movement to encourage negotiations with land owners. This pragmatic mentality of the city government is noticeable throughout Hamburg's history.

---

40 See chapter VII of the urban development contract, available at: https://www.hamburg.de/staedtebaulicher-vertrag/.

The Logics that Shape Hamburg Politics

We identified two intrinsic logics that are reproduced through time in Hamburg: the dissent logic and the Bürger logic. The city government of Hamburg is historically focused on bringing economic prosperity – much like the historic ideal of the Bürger, who was a successful entrepreneur who brought wealth to the city. However, the Bürger logic is not the only logic that is replicated in Hamburg. Activists, outsiders, dreamers and non-conformists invoke the dissent logic to propose new futures for Hamburg. The historically divergent paths of Altona and St. Pauli from Hamburg's once walled centre are still visible in the particularities of the modern day projects. The protest of the *Koordinierungsgremium,* for example, followed Altona's tradition of activism; and the notion of *Schmuddeliger Glamour* reflects the history of the 'freedom' area. These logic patterns highlight the unique politics of Altona and St. Pauli in relation to wider Hamburg, and their focus on economic prosperity. This affects relations between the city government, developers and citizens. Moreover, it affects urban policies and participatory processes. The use of contracts to make deals with developers sidetracked public debate; the municipality uses the Bürger logic to justify these actions, arguing that deals with developers could bring prosperity to the city and benefit many residents. The dissent logic is often used to counter the Bürger logic, and operates on the basis that there is more to politics than the interests of investors or the majority of the residents. Related, the dissent logic values those that defect from the norm and who are not ordinarily in powerful positions. Testament to the tension between dissent and Bürger logics was the Bayerische Hausbau, which due to a lack of sensitivity towards the customs of the neighbourhood, found itself in conflict with the residents of the St. Pauli district. But as the episode neatly illuminates, although embracing the culture of a particular neighbourhood can be time-consuming, it is worthwhile. The result is urban development that is interesting, supported by citizens, and a suitable match for the local area. This also showcases that the dissent logic is not only responsive to the Bürger logic, it is also a creative, inventive force.

The tension between the dissent and Bürger logics of Hamburg creates a space that is inventive and critical but also pragmatic. The members of PlanBude compromised with the Bayerische Hausbau on several occasions. The participatory process of Neue Mitte Altona was heavily criticized, but also resulted in a development project that is barrier-free for people with a disability. The analysis of intrinsic logics has been fruitful in order to understand the characteristics of contemporary Hamburg. Intrinsic logics can help to understand why a participatory process in Altona or St. Pauli will be more contentious than in other parts of the city. However, as our chapter shows, intrinsic logics are also flexible concepts with porous boundaries. They do not fit neatly in every situation, they are concepts in flux that are always adapting: for example, the Bürger logic of Hein Brandt is not the Bürger logic invoked by alderman Andy Grote. But the pull towards economic prosperity and independence, as well as that towards critique and non-conformity helps to understand the institutional setting of Hamburg. Moreover, it helps explain why actors are less radical than in Berlin, or less pragmatic than in Amsterdam. Thus it gives insight in the unique characteristics and the intrinsicness of Hamburg.

Bibliography

Aaslestad, K.B., *Place and Politics: local identity, civic culture, and German nationalism in North Germany during the Revolutionary era* (Leiden and Boston: Brill Academic Publishers, 2005)

Beust, von, O., 'Das Leitbild:"Metropole Hamburg—Wachsende Stadt,"' in: *Wachsende Stadt* (Hamburg: VS Verlag für Sozialwissenschaften, 2004)

Birke, P., 'Herrscht hier Banko? Die aktuellen Proteste gegen das Unternehmen Hamburg', *Sozial. Geschichte Online* (2010) 3, 148-191, 155

Dohnanyi, von, K., 'Unternehmen Hamburg'. Online. Available HTTP: http://www.ueberseeclub.de/resources/Server/pdf-Dateien/1980-1984/vortrag-1983-11-29Dr.%20Klaus%20von%20Dohnanyi.pdf

Freie und Hansestadt Hamburg, 'Städtebaulicher vertrag Neue Mitte Altona', (2014). Online Available HTTP: https://www.hamburg.de/staedtebaulicher-vertrag/.

Freie und Hansestadt Hamburg, BID Projekte, (2021): https://www.hamburg.de/bid-projekte/.

Freie und Hansestadt Hamburg, DIPAS, (2021): https://www.hamburg.de/dipas/.

Freie und Hansestadt Hamburg, 'Behörde für Stadtentwicklung und Wohnen' *Hamburger Projekte der Stadtentwicklung 2015-2030* (2019). Online. Available HTTP:https://www.hamburg.de/stadtplanung/projekte/.

Freie und Hansestadt Hamburg, 'Räumliches Leitbild Entwurf: Wachsende Stadt - Grüne Metropole am Wasser', (2007)

Friedrich, J., 'Social inequality, segregation and urban conflict: the case of Hamburg', in: S. Musterd and W. Ostendorf (eds.) *Urban Segregation and the Welfare State: Inequality and exclusion in western cities* (London and New York: Routledge, 1998) 191–206

Fux: https://www.fux-eg.org/

Gassdorf, U and Fischer, M. 'Prominente Abrissgegner', *Die Welt*, 2013

Hurd, M., *Public Spheres, Public Mores, and Democracy Hamburg and Stockholm, 1870-1914* (Ann Arbor: The University of Michigan Press, 2000)

Kaiser, L., 'Kein Abriss ohne Kompromiss', *Die Tageszeitung*, 9 February 2012

Koordinierungsgremium Mitte Altona, 'Ein Moratorium für Mitte Altona', (2012)

Levine, J.R., 'The paradox of community power: cultural processes and elite authority in participatory governance', *Social Forces* (2017) 95(3), 1155–1179

Lindemann, M., *The merchant republics: Amsterdam, Antwerp, and Hamburg, 1648-1790* (New York: Cambridge University Press, 2015)

Manos, H., *Sankt Pauli : soziale Lagen und soziale Fragen im Stadtteil Sankt Pauli* (Hamburg: Ergebnisse, 1989)

Novy, J. and Colomb, C., 'Struggling for the right to the (creative) city in Berlin and Hamburg: New urban social movements, new "spaces of hope"?', *International Journal of Urban and Regional Research* (2013) 37(5), 1816–1838

Park-Fiction. Online. Available HTTP: https://park-fiction.net/

Planbude, 'St. Pauli Code', (2015). Online. Available HTTP: https://planbude.de/st-pauli-code/

Q8, 'Konkretisierung inklusiver Strukturen in Mitte Altona: Empfehlungen des Forums Eine Mitte für Alle', (2015)

Rodenstein, M., 'Die Eigenart der Städte – Frankfurt und Hamburg im Vergleich', in: M. Löw and H. Berking, *Die Eigenlogik der Städte* (Frankfurt and New York: Campus, 2008) 261-311

Rodnick, D., *A Portrait of Two German Cities: Lübeck and Hamburg* (Lubbock, Texas: The Caprock Press, 1980)

St.Pauli Selber Machen: https://www.st-pauli-selber-machen.de/ballsaal-resolution/

Verg, E. and Verg, M., *Das Abenteuer das Hamburg heißt* (4th ed.), (Hamburg: Ellert&Richter, 2007)

Vogelpohl, A., 'McKinseyisierung oder Regierungsprojekt? Unternehmensberatungen in der strategischen Stadtentwicklung. Das Beispiel „Metropole Hamburg – Wachsende Stadt", Raumforschung und Raumordnung (2017) 75, 327–338

Zentner, C. and Bedürftig, F., *The encyclopedia of the third reich* (New York: Macmillan, 1991)

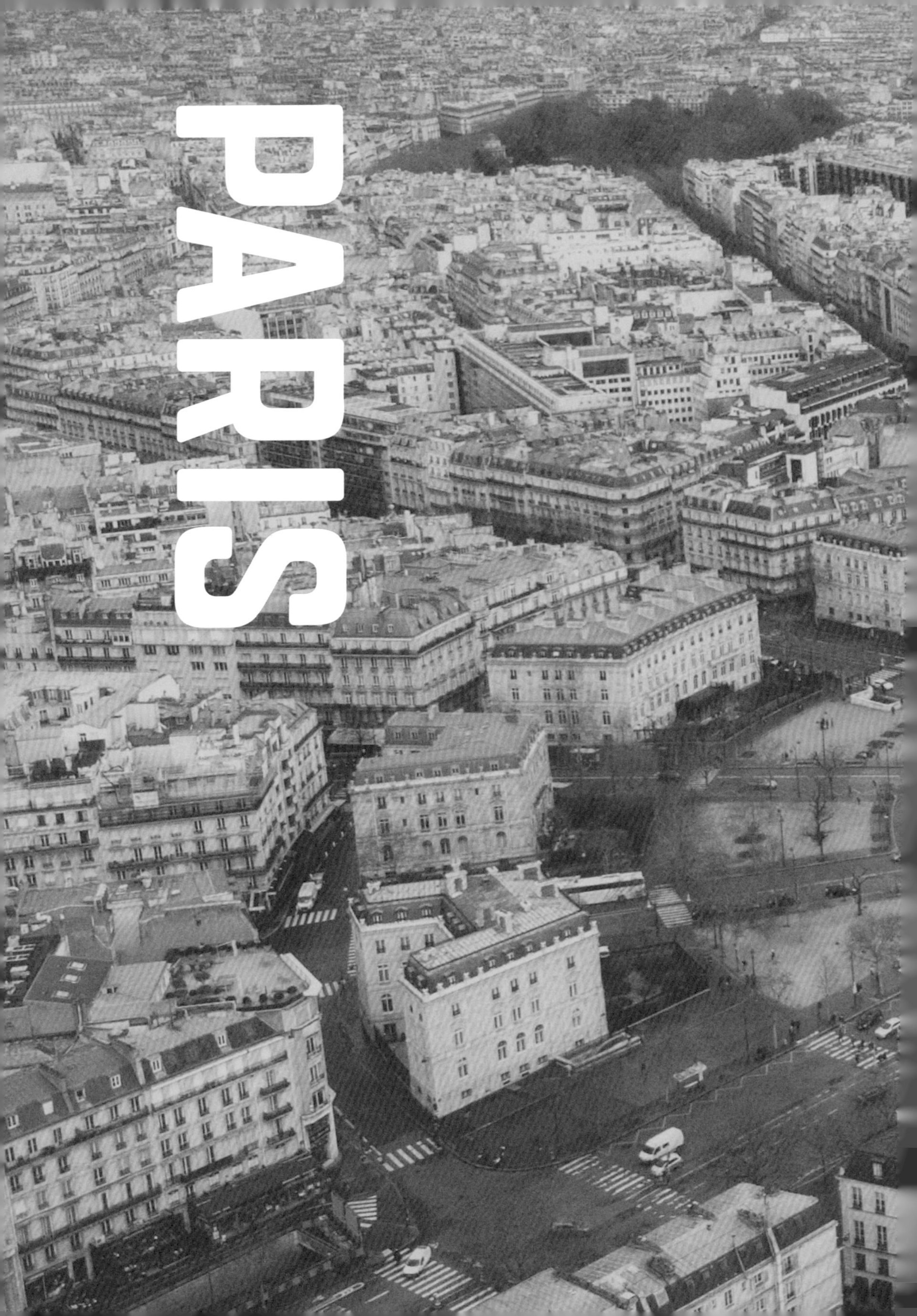
PARIS

Paris: The All-Encompassing City

Menno van der Veen and Jan Willem Duyvendak

When one has studied Paris for a while, they are likely to become dazzled by its myriad dimensions and vast range of urban policies. Above all, it is a city of duality: a capital both of richness and extreme poverty, it is also known for its violent protests and peaceful public debates. It is at once the archetypical city of lights — as well as the setting of Matthieu Kassovitz's 1995 film, *La Haine*,[1] which depicts conflicts between the police and the youth of the *banlieue*.[2] Paris is a chic city that builds temples for highbrow culture as it celebrates the bohemian. It is both a monument for the cultural and political history of France, and a showcase for groundbreaking architecture spanning the modern — the Eiffel tower, for example — and post-modern, such as the iconic Centre Pompidou that transformed a district.

Readers of the work of Marcel Proust may have come to know Paris as a city that operates as much behind closed doors, shaped by elites, as it does in the open. Indeed, there are those who argue that this particular trait is far from confined to Proust's Belle Époque, and that its echoes could still be found in the late-twentieth century 'cohabitation' between Jacques Chirac and François Mitterrand.[3,4] Despite the former leaning right and the latter, left, the concurrent mayor and

1 *La Haine*, dir. by Mathieu Kassovitz (Canal+, 1995)

2 In francophone areas, *banlieues* are the outskirts of a city: the zone around a city that is not necessarily under the city's jurisdiction. *Banlieues* are most commonly translated as 'suburbs.'

3 Jacques Chirac (1932-2019) was Mayor of Paris from 1977 to 1995. After he served as President of France from 1995 to 2007.

4 Chirac's predecessor was François Mitterrand (1916-1996), President of France from 1981-1995.

president recognized in each other in a shared ambition to make Paris a world capital once again.

But Paris is also known for its 'revolutionary' attitude. If the population feels that it is mistreated by its rulers, it will rise up against them. Case in point: the French Revolution of 1789 that resulted in the expropriation of all clergy buildings; and the student-led protests of May 1968 that put a halt to Modernist redevelopment. In the twenty-first century, Paris has seen violent protests by inhabitants of its poorest neighborhoods against marginalization: in 2005, youth of African and Arab heritage rioted for three weeks in protest against police harassment and unemployment, with burning cars becoming a symbol of the uprising. More recently were the 'yellow jacket' protests of 2018 which emphasized distributive justice. All point to France's spiralling dynamics between social movements on the one hand, and government responses on the other. Paris, as the capital of a highly centralized state, is a global stage for protests that have at times inspired people across the world.

In this century, Paris has also been the stage of horrific terrorist attacks, including that at the offices of satirical newspaper, Charlie Hebdo in January 2015; and in November of the same year, at the Bataclan Theater.

These uprisings and attacks all have left their imprints on modern Paris and paved the way for draconian anti-terrorism measures, but also for new democratic initiatives.

Paris is a planned city. Unlike its world-city siblings like London and New York, it is not about spontaneity, but rather about grandeur — be it of its projects, policies or ambitions. Its Eigenlogik is that of an all-encompassing city,[5] a quintessential world-city that combines the features of being recognizably French in every aspect with those of a global metropolis. It is a city that stands out as much for its monuments as its modernity; its high-brow culture as its underground scenes; its wealth as its inclusive policies; and for its presidential interventions as much as its bottom-up approaches to planning in poor neighborhoods.

In practice, Paris' aim of being all-encompassing brings with it various tensions and paradoxes. Through these tensions emerges a portrait of a city that is

---

5 M. Löw, *Soziologie der Städte Berlin:* (Berlin: Suhrkamp Verlag, 2013)

constantly seeking to plan for everything while encountering many challenges that are hard to handle. Historically, this has been evidenced by its rulers' grand urban development projects that focused on desired outcomes, not on the process of participation. Some of these projects were done with the interests of the Paris public in mind, such as the construction of city parks like the Bois de Boulogne and Parc des Buttes-Chaumont in the nineteenth century. Others were realized for the benefit of the city's future, like Emperor Napoléon III commissioning of Haussmann's large-scale urban renovation of Paris to replace the medieval structure of the city with large boulevards. Although the intervention forced thousands from their homes, it also reduced pollution and rendered the city more fit for growth. Other projects still were carried out for the pleasure of French kings, such as the Louvre: a museum since the late-eighteenth century, in its thousand-year history the site has also been a fortress for the treasures of King Philip II, and a primary royal residence for several of his descendants. And of course, some projects were more for image sake — like the Eiffel Tower's symbolization of Paris as a modern city at the end of the nineteenth century.

Participation

Participation can be defined as a set of procedural goals — that is, equal access to processes — and as a set of desired outcomes (such as more inclusive policies). How then is the Eigenlogik of Paris as an all-encompassing city reflected in citizen participation? Since the early 2000s, Paris has been slowly re-inventing itself as a city that prides itself on including local residents in its planning processes. This is happening on several levels: firstly, Paris is opening up its participation policies to make these more inclusive, effectively giving a broader variety of people a seat at the table. But it is also seeking ways to make the outcomes of participation processes more inclusive, by engaging in new approaches to ultimately cater to diverse interest groups.

This includes re-thinking how the city works with *associations*: non-profit making clubs or charities, *la vie associative* (the association sector) is a vital element of French society. In addition to working towards participation based on proximity (that is, who lives nearby), positive engagement with *associations* can open up participation processes for more people.

The city is also trying to find a balance between wide-ranging inclusiveness and catering to specific groups. This is illustrated by various examples of the redevelopment of obsolete buildings that provide working spaces for artists, and also function as community centers.

The Paris planning system

Marco Cremaschi, Professor of Urban Politics at the Sciences Po University in Paris, observes that Paris functions as an 'all-encompassing political system.'[6] His assessment provides useful context for understanding the city's planning policies. In Cremaschi's view there are hardly any areas of citizen initiatives for which no policy exists. 'If an artist turns up at Rue de Rivoli, the next day there will be a "Rue de Rivoli Art Policy" to ensure that all interests are dealt with, including those of the artist,' he said. Cremaschi contrasts Paris with his experiences in Italy, where fewer policies mean that this hypothetical artist could in all likelihood stay – albeit in a sort of legal and planning limbo – until he was moved on by the police.

Another important characteristic of Parisian urban planning policy is the strict distinction to be made between Paris and Greater Paris, or metropolitan area. The city proper comprises 20 administrative districts (known as *arrondissements)*, contained with the Boulevard Périphérique ring road. Home to an estimated 2.4 million inhabitants, it is the densest city in the European Union. The other Paris, also known as *Île-de-France,*[7] covers vast swathes of far-flung suburbs and is home to around 11 million. The distinction not only reflects the difference between the city and its suburbs, but also the difference between the city that is (more or less) completed and has not much space left to build and the suburbs that are not. It is also in this context that lies one of Paris' starkest dualities: the divide between one of the most expensive cities in the world, and the poverty of its suburbs. These concurrent realities also point to a historical mindset whose effects still resonate today: the authorities have traditionally focused on the center and showed little interest in the needs and opportunities of the outskirt areas.

Although part of the national planning system since the end of World War Two, Paris' size, governance and complexity make it a unique case. Before the Second

---

6 Marco Cremaschi, in conversation with the authors, April 2018

7 Literally translated to 'Island of France' and the most populous of the 18 administrative regions of France. 90 per cent of the region is covered by the *Aire Urbaine Parisienne* (Metropolitan Area of Paris), which reaches beyond its borders at some locations.

World War, Parisian planners worked under the auspices of the Seine Prefecture and were largely occupied with slum clearance. Right after, housing constituted the city's central planning crisis and challenge, resulting in higher-density construction in the urban periphery. This was facilitated by the 1955 Urban Renewal Law, which gave the Municipal Council power to declare parts of the city substandard. Planning staff of the Prefecture were then authorized to redevelop those areas for higher and better uses. Factory districts, warehouses, port facilities and quays, as well as low-density residential areas were all redeveloped based on this planning instrument. In total, the Urban Renewal Law resulted in around 12 square kilometers in the city center – almost 25 per cent of its buildable surface – being redeveloped along Modernist principles. They included the area surrounding Place d'Italie in the 13th *arrondissement,* which was reorganized into multiple high-rise towers so as to free up ground space. A similar approach can be seen in the 15th *arrondissement* by way of the 212-metre-tall Tour de Montparnasse.

The 1960s were significant in terms of Paris' development and discussions surrounding its built environment. In this decade, the city's characteristic tensions between planned and revolutionary; and the center and the suburbs once again came to the fore. In 1965 a new regional plan was made. Three years later, in the aftermath of May 1968, residents mobilized to protest the demolishing and rebuilding of the old city.

In 1977, Jacques Chirac was elected as the first Mayor of Paris in more than 100 years, after the post was abolished in the late nineteenth century. When socialist François Mitterrand won the French presidency in 1981, the two became unlikely allies, with Chirac going on to become Prime Minister under Mitterrand in 1986.

In 1982 Mitterrand notably launched the architectural program, *Grands Projets*, also known as *Grands Travaux.* Essentially a series of new high-profile buildings, the scheme was intended to renovate and revitalize the national heritage in the sphere of culture and its relationship with the universal,' explained former Secretary of State for the *Grands Projets*, Emile Biasini in a 1991 lecture.[8] Specifically initiated to revitalize the grandeur of Paris on the national and world stage, and motivated by the upcoming bicentennial of France in 1989, Mitterrand announced his *Grand Projets* as the national library, the new business district La Défense (with its new Grand Arche), and the Opéra Bastille. These large state

8 E.J. Biasini, *Les Grands Projets: an Overview*, Bossom Lectures, 18 March 1991.

interventions in planning aligned with the more neoliberal policies of Chirac who aimed to raise property value by investing in infrastructure and decreasing rules and regulations.

From an economic point of view, the successes of these interventions depend on making smart use of the city's 'amenities'. The city's 'historical monuments, parks, boulevards, fine architecture, and river scenery give central Paris a large amenity advantage over the suburbs. If the amenity demand of the rich is strong enough, such an advantage might be sufficient to draw rich households to central locations.[9] In other words, the *Grand Projets* helped to add more value to the real estate in the old center.

The *Grands Projets* do not only highlight divisions between the suburbs and the centre. Within the city's 20 *arrondissements,* they also underline discrepancies between the northern and southern parts of Paris. Indeed, a mainstay of the capital's most significant monuments and developments are to be found in the city's south: the Eiffel Tower and the Rive Gauche development, for example.

All that began to change in 2001 on the election of left-wing Mayor Bertrand Delanoë, who shifted the focus of policies from south of the Seine to north. That meant a redistribution of cultural amenities and infrastructure to other parts of the city. One such example is a new center for police and justice buildings (*la cité judiciaire de Paris*) opened in Batignolles which is in the 17th arrondissement. Another example of the broader focus of Paris planning is the construction of the Grand Paris Express. An investment in the region of 20 billion Euros, it comprises 200 kilometers of new subway tracks to better connect the city's outskirts with its center, and promote economic development in the Greater Paris area.[10] Mayor Delanoë also put more emphasis on the construction of social housing by implementing policies to buy property and subsidizing landlords.

---

9 J.K. Brueckner, J.F. Thisse, Y. Zenou, Y (1999). 'Why is Central Paris Rich and Downtown Detroit Poor? An Amenity-Based Theory', *European Economic Review* (1999) vol. 43(1), 94: '. . . where exogenous amenities decline rapidly with distance to the center, might correspond to Paris. Its historical monuments, parks, boulevards, fine architecture, and river scenery give central Paris a large amenity advantage over the suburbs. If the amenity demand of the rich is strong enough, such an advantage might be sufficient to draw rich households to central locations . . .'
10 X. Desjardins. 'Greater Paris and its Lessons for Metropolitan Strategic Planning', *Town Planning Review* (2018), 89(1), 1

In the arts, urban sociologist Elsa Vivant notes a shift in Paris between what she describes as 'in culture' and 'off culture.'[11] The former describes established platforms such as opera houses, concert halls, theatres, newspapers, galleries and exhibitions. 'Off culture' alludes more to informality, temporal use of space, new types of music, and street art. Vivant notes that Paris now invests more funds in 'off culture' than it does more traditional formats, citing nighttime arts festival, 'Nuit Blanche,' that was introduced in 2002.[12] This shift of focus was continued by Mayor Anne Hidalgo who replaced Delanoë in 2014.

Some Key Elements of Urban Planning in Paris

An important element of the Paris planning system is that of zoning for specific projects. Known as the ZAC – or *Zone d'Aménagement Concerté* – it is a defined development zone that is often managed by a semi-public company (SEM) and a special board. For the ZAC, a development plan (*plan d'aménagement de zone*) is made that until the year 2000, made them exempt from the Parisian and national planning systems. Since 2000 these plans have to be integrated in the PLU (see below) and comply with city regulations. Most of the *Grand Projets* in Paris are situated within a ZAC.[13]

Like all French cities, Paris is required to make a binding land use plan, or *Plan Local d'Urbanisme* (PLU). In addition, France has a policy practice called *Politique de la Ville* which effectively allows cities to designate specific zones that are in need of a cohesive approach of social, economic and spatial measures. The policy also involves a specific type of contracting: *Contrat de Ville* requires cities to enter into a 'contract' with the collective representatives (*associations*) of the city. These contracts are required in order to receive government funding for the zones in need of these measures. In Paris, the *Contrat de Ville 2015-2020* resulted in

---

11 E. Vivant, E. (2009). 'How Underground Culture is Changing Paris', *Urban Research & Practice* (2009) vol 2, 39–44
12 Vivant, 'Underground Culture', op. cit. (note 11), 45
13 Heathcott, J., 'The Promenade Plantée: Politics, Planning, and Urban Design in Postindustrial Paris', *Journal of Planning Education and Research* (2013) 33(3), 280–291

the designation of 20 new priority neighbourhoods to receive money for measures regarding their regeneration.[14]

The most important government actor in Paris is the city council that sets the budget and decides on the PLU. Within that, Paris consists of 20 *arrondissements* that each have their own council and mayor. It is the mayors who design territorial plans regarding their respective constituencies. Zooming in further still, within each *arrondissement* are neighbourhood councils: constituting a mixture of local residents, *associations* and appointees of the local mayor, the aim of these neighbourhood bodies is to promote participation of citizens in their area. Their influence is mostly based on their expertise and their right to be consulted. They do not have the authority to take or confirm planning decisions.

An important institution of Paris is the *Atelier Parisien d'Urbanisme* that was created in 1967. This non-profit organization consists of 27 partner members in the Paris regions. Its main task is to conduct studies and propose plans for the development of Paris.[15]

Property and Developers

The French Revolution re-shaped the city's property structure: prior to the uprising approximately half of the city was owned by the clergy. Today, it is about 0.3 per cent.[16] The French state owns some of the best-known monuments and parks in Paris, including the Louvre Museum and the Jardin du Luxembourg. In addition, the city of Paris owns about 9 per cent of buildings – approximately 7,800 – and in recent years has sought to acquire more in order to realize its goals of mixed housing. Paris is under some pressure of foreign investment (7 per cent of the real estate transactions in 2012). Most of the city's residential property comprises of co-ownership of apartment buildings (more than 50 per cent, or 48,439 buildings).

---

14 *Direction Departmentale de la Cohesion Sociale de Paris* (2014). Online. Available HTTP: http://www.ddcs.paris.gouv.fr/SITE-DDCS/Politique-de-la-ville-Egalite-des-chances/Politique-de-la-ville/Contrat-de-ville-2015-2020

15 https://www.apur.org

16 Paris Property Group, 'Who Owns Paris Real Estate?', *This Paris Life*. Online. Available HTTP: https://parispropertygroup.com/blog/2013/owns-paris-real-estate/ (accessed 17 February 2021).

Although these figures point to large parts of Paris being owned by (relatively) small owners, in many of its development projects the city is still a relevant and sometimes primary actor.[17] Because land in Paris is expensive and ownership sprawled, development projects are often complex to realize as there are many land-owners involved. Large developers also play a very important role. Some of the best known are Hine, which is responsible for La Défense; Bouygues in Clichy Batignolles; and Icade, which is one of the largest owners of office space and business parks in the city and also active in the healthcare sector. As participation processes in Paris are mostly directed to public decision makers, a particular challenge is to also involve this private sector in its outcomes.

Paris as a tourist destination and Innovative center

Paris is one of the world's most popular destinations for international tourism: in 2019, its particular combination of culture, fashion, and 'old world charm' attracted more than 40 million foreign visitors.[18] But this projection of a city steeped in tradition is also a burden: to international investors, Paris is oftentimes viewed as a site of government, big companies and old industries, and lacking the vibrancy necessary for new economic developments. For this reason, President Macron stated in 2017 that he wanted France to be a 'startup nation.'[19] Certainly, the current Mayor of Paris, Hidalgo, has invested in an image of 'green development' and a startup economy. She prides herself in promoting 'incubators, co-working spaces and fabrication labs.' In 2014, for example, she launched urban initiative, *Reinventer Paris* that sought innovative redevelopment solutions for 23 buildings across the city, equating to around 150,000 square metres. A second edition of the competition, *Réinventer Paris - Les dessous de Paris* focused on 33 underground sites, including the Tuileries Tunnel, and was launched in 2017. Another initiative was that of Paris Green a cooperation between the city's climate agency and the agency *Paris Développement* that promotes foreign investment and the city's worldwide economic development. Paris Green, which is now part

17 Desjardins, 'Lessons for Metropolitan Strategic Planning', op. cit. (note 10)

18 C. Rabbiosi, 'Renewing a Historical Legacy: Tourism, Leisure Shopping and Urban Branding in Paris' *Cities* (2015) 42, Part B, 195–203

19 E.J.M.F. Macron, 'Entrepreneur is the New France, *Viva Technology* (conference), 15 June 2017.

of climate agency *Agence Parisienne du Climat*, aims to promote the city's climate goals through financing and creative solutions. Describing how the initiative would impact an eco-district within the 17th *arrondissement* of Clichy-Batignolles, founder of Paris-based planning consultancy, Une Autre Ville, Nicolas Rougé, wrote, 'The authorities here are setting their sights higher than ever before by aiming to be a model of energy efficiency in the fight against climate change.'[20] The Clichy-Batignolles site will house 7,500 people and more than 12,000 jobs.[21] In other words, Paris is looking for ways to present itself not as 'one of the museum cities' of the world, but as an attractive, sustainable, and innovative metropole.

But what is the role of inhabitants in this process? The function of citizen participation in the context of these strategies is not so much about discussing with the local community what will and what will not be built. Instead, citizen participation is envisaged as providing room for small groups of entrepreneurs that need spaces to work in. An initiative is welcomed when it is backed by a feasible financial strategy, not because it is the outcome of a participation process.[22]

On the other hand, some the spaces for these initiatives are often found in locations that also cater for less profitable functions. Take, for example, cultural center the Cent Quatre, located in the Paris neighborhood of Aubervilliers in the 19th *arrondissement*. A former funeral house commissioned by the Archbishop of Paris in the late eighteenth century, it was renovated in 2008. Today, it houses artist spaces and galleries, a business incubator, and also runs community engagement and working experience programs. The center is a good example of planning for complex buildings that aim to generate economic value by combining various uses and public areas.[23] The project Les Grands Voisins (see below) also stands out for combining profitable and non-profitable uses, and creating private and public accessible areas.

---

20 N. Rougé and U.A. Vilie, 'Clichy-Batignolles: Where Urban Planning Meets the Climate'. *OECD Observer* (2015) 304, 53

21 S. Shmurak, 'Here's how Paris is Building the Eco-Community of the Future', *GreenBiz* (2018) Online. Available HTTP:https://www.greenbiz.com/article/heres-how-paris-building-eco-community-future (accessed 17 February 2021)

22 C. Tardieu, 'Transition énergétique dans les projets urbains: conditions de mise en œuvre. Analyse des cas Paris Rive Gauche, Clichy-Batignolles et Paris Nord Est', doctoral dissertation, (2015), Université Lille1

23 R. D'Autilia and J. Hetman, 'Complex Buildings and Cellular Automata—A Cellular Automaton Model for the Centquatre-Paris'. *Urban Science* (2018), 2(2), 50

Thus, although the process by which these initiatives are being initiated may feel somewhat exclusive (or not democratic), its desired outcomes are very much aligned with the idea of inclusiveness that is typical for the all-encompassing approach to urban planning of Paris.

Interest groups and local residents

In an interview, sociologist Tommaso Vitale said that the city's focus on *associations* over neighborhoods is quintessentially Parisian.[24] He commented that in Italy, a neighborhood festival will likely simply target those who live locally; in Paris, because organizers may represent groups spanning everything from the bicycle association to the parents' association, the focus of activity becomes more specific to these particular groups. Categorical *associations*, he noted, are less inclusive than those based on territory.

With regard to participation, Paris has recently started initiatives and experiments to cater for both of these approaches. That is to say, participation based on the principle of proximity, while not excluding the more focused perspective of *associations*. It should be noted that these experiments are not unique to Paris, and are being initiated across all of France.

Rive Gauche: The Power of Associations

A telling example of the power of *associations* in Paris is the redevelopment of Rive Gauche. The Rive Gauche is a *Grand Projet* situated in four zones of the 13th *arrondissement*: Austerlitz railway station, the Bibliothèque National de France (Tolbiac), the Paris 7 University (Masséna) and the Boulevard Périphérique (Bruneseau). It spans approximately 130 hectares, 26 of which are above Austerlitz station.
Starting in the 1990s, the aim of this *Grand Projet* was to redevelop an obsolete industrial site into a mixed zone of public and commercial buildings, as well housing and new green sites. It is famously stated to be the largest-scale project since the works of Hausmann in the nineteenth century.

---

24 Tommaso Vitale, in conversation with the authors, March 2017 and March 2018

The sociologist Héloise Nez who specializes in participatory democracy interestingly points out that the project shows some of the difficulties of the Paris approach to organizing participation. Citizen involvement in Paris is based on the principles of 'intimate knowledge' and 'proximity.' [25] This means that citizens are asked for their opinions and have a right to participate because of their knowledge of the local circumstances and their proximity in a literal sense. Therefore, she points out, the *Grand Projets* of Paris lack a system of citizen participation as these big transformational projects are of national importance and therefore not defined in terms of 'intimacy and proximity.' However, this is where the *associations* come in. For the participation component of the Rive Gauche redevelopment, a total of 26 *associations* were engaged with the project.[26] These *associations* joined forces and the project now is mostly known for the work of ADA 13, a local *association* that voiced the interests of the (poor) neighborhood population; and Tam-Tam that was named after three of development's zones (Tolbiac-Austerlitz-Masséna) and created specifically for the project. The two *associations* claimed that the plan lacked citizen participation by excluding local residents, placing too much emphasis on business interests through extensive office space, prioritized car use, had insufficient green areas and lacked a Hausmann-style vision on city development instead focusing on isolated towers that were barely connected to their surroundings.

Because of the local and political contacts and expertise of these *associations*, the plan changed significantly. Specifically, its focus shifted from car-heavy infrastructure, and green spaces were doubled to 100,000 square meters. Intervention from the *associations* helped diminish the amount of office space from 900,000 square meters to 745,000 square meters, and increase space for housing from 520,000 square meters to 585,000 square meters. It therefore seems reasonable to conclude that the work of the two *associations* made a big difference for the project.

---

25 H. Nez, 'De l'expertise associative à la constitution d'un contre-pouvoir. Action collective et concertation à Paris Rive Gauche', *Espaces et Sociétés*, *3*(1), 139–154.
26 Nez, 'De l'expertise associative', op. cit (note 25), 148

Les Grands Voisins: Opening Up an Obsolete Site for Everybody

An interesting recent case was Les Grands Voisins, which shut its doors in September 2020 to make way for a new housing development. Managed by *associations*, like the Cent Quatre project it provided private spaces for specific groups as well as public spaces and activities. Variously described through its five-year history as a 'cooperative village' or even 'urban oasis,' it was particularly successful in bringing together multiple types of users.

Les Grands Voisins was situated on an obsolete hospital site of four hectares in the 14th *arrondissement*. It combined housing for immigrants with artists residences and galleries. It also hosted a small campsite within its walls, as well as a hotel, co-working space, a small cinema, café and restaurant. It was managed by *association* for homeless people, Aurore; Plateau Urbain, an organization that specializes in temporary use of vacant buildings; and Yes We Camp that focuses on city campsites and hospitality.

In 2017 we interviewed Dickel Bokoum of Yes We Camp. In her view, the most interesting part of the site was that it offered urban, and for visitors, recognizable functions — such as a bar with local foods and beers, campsite, urban farming, bees and art galleries — with a very open attitude towards the neighborhood and visitors. It combined these functions with the reintegration of homeless people who worked on the site, selling food. But at the same time, as Bokoum stated, the site was 'above all, a place of living.' The seamless integration of public functions and shelter for the homeless came down to smart design. This included a clear signage system diverting visitors from areas designated for residents of the shelter. Another example was what Bokoum described as 'soft programming.' By this she meant that music and performances were not aggressive, and stopped at 11pm.

Dorian Carreau-Touzé who worked at the project and also wrote his master's thesis on it points to the ambitious governance structure of Les Grands Voisins.[27] It was characterized by a hybrid of decision making and consultation, based on the frameworks that were given by institutional partners (such as the city and

---

27 D. Carreau-Touzé, Connecter des espaces sans personnes à des personnes sans espaces les Grands Voisins, un lieu infini, master thesis, (2019), Université Paris 1 Panthéon-Sorbonne.

the boards of the NGOs), as well as the voiced opinions of the neighborhood. This resulted in three key working committees — Technics and Space, Social Work, and Programming and Art — that collectively oversaw the various activities of Les Grands Voisins.

In this way, Les Grands Voisins' aim of connecting people and creating a new urban experience moved beyond merely a hipster pipe dream. After being granted a temporary contract to manage the area in 2015, this was prolonged in 2018 until finally being terminated in 2020 to make room for new development.

Finding new ways to include everybody

In 2006, Paris adapted a Consultation Charter. This charter introduced the requirement of involving representatives of local people, project designers and owners in thematic groups. These were called *Groupes de Travail Thématiques.* However, the good intentions of this charter fail to acknowledge that the deliberation process of designers and politicians follows its own schedules, and that in order to make the concertation process meaningful it should be adapted to that planning. In addition, the concertation process does not directly acknowledge the public-private nature of most development projects.

Still the adaptation of the charter can be seen as recognition that the well-managed political system of institutionalized consultation and deliberation only works for those who know how to access it. In 2017 we interviewed Julien Antelin who worked as Mayor Hidalgo's Chief of Staff and oversaw Paris' participatory budget program from 2014 until 2016. Antelin emphasized the problem of representativeness. *Associations* know how to make their voice heard, but who are represented by these *associations*? Ultimately, these organizations tend to cater to specific interests, and no matter their level of engagement, many Parisians do not feel represented by them. He is also critical of neighborhood councils — *conseils de quartiers* — that were introduced in 2002 and are organized by the mayor of the *arrondissements*, and required for neighborhoods of more than 80,000 inhabitants.[28] Rather than being chosen, members are appointed by the mayor. Given a small budget, their intended role is to advise on all topics that are of importance

---

28 J. Demoulin and M-H. Bacqué, 'Les conseils citoyens, beaucoup de bruit pour rien?' *Participations* (2019) no. 24(2), 5

to the neighborhood. In Antelin's view, these councils attract a specific — and usually older — type of councillor and fail to represent the wider population of their respective neighborhoods.

As for new forms of participation, Paris has also experimented with various digital democracy tools and has reserved a respectable part of its budget for participatory purposes. The participatory budget was introduced in 2014 by Mayor Hidalgo, with the pledge to spend 500 million Euros in six years on residents' proposals. Paris claims that it thereby has the largest participatory budget of all western cities.

Proposals are made to the city council, which must then approve them as part of the budget reserved for the *arrondissements,* or of its own budget. To that end, there are 21 participatory budgets in total. That comprises one per *arrondissement,* with the winner of each seeing their proposed investment tripled by the city. Another is for the city as a whole. In addition, there is also a competition aimed specifically at children.

Theoretically, the participatory budgets process offers a chance for everybody to realize their idea. In practice, however, it is *associations* that are responsible for many of the winning proposals, as they know how to mobilize members' knowledge, professional expertise, and network. A case in point is Paris-en-Seine which is an *association* that aims to promote cycling, created because of the participatory budget process.

Reflecting on some of the challenges of the participatory budgets program, Antelin describes the initiative as being implemented more or less overnight. Quite simply, his team was not ready to deal with the 5,000 or so proposals that it received. Over time, more voting ballots were placed and the city actively encouraged initiators of similar proposals to join forces, as this would improve their chances of success. He also states that the participatory budget process introduced a new type of direct democracy, therefore creating tensions with the neighborhood councils that are, in a certain sense, bypassed when projects are being granted. As to the type of projects submitted and their impact on the city, many of the proposals fit the city's goals such as improving cycling infrastructure or environmental sustainability.

Whereas the participatory budget is about finding votes for specific projects, the *conseils citoyens,* or citizen councils, are about involving more residents in policies and neighborhood initiatives. Aimed at ensuring participation among residents of the city's lowest-income neighborhoods (or *quartiers prioritaires*), these councils comprise half local *associations* and half residents. The latter group is selected at random by address, and strives for a balance between men and women. In Paris, where a significant proportion of the population do not have a French passport and effectively exist outside of most institutional systems, this is especially important. After all, they also greatly contribute to the city and its livability.[29]

Nevertheless, experts opine that the impact of citizen councils is very limited. Although members are residents, they are often not linked to *associations* and therefore lack know-how and knowledge of planning systems, and the content of new plans. Simply, they are neither sufficiently well-connected or trained. As a result, they are often bypassed or will discuss only minor details of a plan.

In conclusion, although citizen councils are ostensibly successful in attracting a new member type, their impact is limited in comparison to the connections and resources of *associations*.

Les Halles: The Participation Challenges of Large-Scale Projects

Like most Western metropoles, Paris is also experiencing the increasing influence of the private sector. How can participation then be directed to projects that are dominated by both the public and the private sectors?

One of the most noticeable redevelopment projects in Paris is that of Les Halles between 2010 and 2016. The famous market was demolished in 1971, and now houses a public garden, shopping center, as well as the city's busiest subway station.

---

29 Y. Cabannes, 'Participatory Budgeting in Paris: Act, Reflect, Grow', in: Y. Cabannes (ed.) *Another City Is Possible with Participatory Budgeting* (Montréal/New York/London: Black Rose Books, 2017), 179-203.

The concertation process was followed by urban sociologist Camille Gardesse.[30] In her analysis, she points to the typical tensions that come with the various interests involved in the project. Although not known as a best practice — despite its design competition attracting worldwide attention — the project is representative of the many issues of public participation in Paris. These include local versus city or national levels; the associations versus the non-organized; the political domain and the domain of citizen participation; public versus private.

Parisians could vote for the news designs of the Les Halles project (about 14,000 people did). However, the broad concertation process that was promised never took place as the process focused on organizations and institutional actors. On behalf of citizens, only *associations* were invited to express their views. Local residents could only participate on a neighborhood level. Therefore, despite the option to vote for the final designs, the influence of inhabitants on the actual design choices was very limited.

The concertation process of Les Halles was carried out by the Paris Centre SEM. However, negotiations with construction companies and institutional partners were separated from the concertation process. Therefore, it is hard to pinpoint the influence of the Paris population, or of the neighborhood.

The Les Halles project in this respect brings to light the difficulties that come with organizing a meaningful participation process that deals with mega-infrastructures. How to synchronize the public deliberation process including politicians and civil servants on the one hand, and non-political actors such as *associations*, property owners and residents on the other? Arguably, Paris has not yet found an answer to the public-private nature of most large development projects. To a great extent, the concertation process is still very much centered around the idea of political decision making.[31]

---

30 C. Gardesse, 'The fraught 'menage à trois' of public actors, private players and inhabitants: Problems of participation in French urban development projects', *Urban Studies* (2015) 52(16), 3035–3053
31 Gardesse, 'Problems of participation', op. cit. (note 30), 3043

Conclusion

Paris has many lessons and insights to offer regarding citizen involvement and urban development. In this city of all-encompassing ambitions, various tensions between the local and the metropolitan can be found. All the while, Paris continues to reinvent itself as a green, innovative metropole, hailing a new, less centralistic perspective on the city and with new types of participation. The most interesting projects we encountered in Paris seek to combine the interests of 'creatives' that look for new dynamic places in their neighborhoods, with the urgent needs of the precariat. Rive Gauche stands out as an example of how *associations* managed to negotiate a better deal for Parisians and the local neighborhood by making well-informed proposals to change the development plans.

However, the city seems to fall short of finding new ways to direct participation towards the private and public-private entities that are gaining importance in the city's development strategies — as they are in many other cities. Last but not least: even though new forms of citizen participation are being continually tested, an ongoing challenge is to include less well-organized, more marginal citizens.

Bibliography:

Brueckner, J. K., Thisse, J. F., & Zenou, Y., 'Why is central Paris rich and downtown Detroit poor? An amenity-based theory', *European Economic Review*, vol 43(1) (1999).

Cabannes, Y., 'Participatory Budgeting in Paris: Act, Reflect, Grow', in Y. Cabannes (ed): *Another City Is Possible with Participatory Budgeting* (Montréal/New York/London: Black Rose Books, 2017).

Carreau-Touzé, D., Connecter des espaces sans personnes à des personnes sans espaces : les Grands Voisins, un lieu infini, master thesis (2019), Université Paris 1 Panthéon-Sorbonne.

D'Autilia, R. and Hetman, J., 'Complex Buildings and Cellular Automata—A Cellular Automaton Model for the Centquatre-Paris'. *Urban Science* (2018) 2(2).

Demoulin, J. and Bacqué, M-H., 'Les conseils citoyens, beaucoup de bruit pour rien?' *Participations* (2019) No. 24(2)

Desjardins, X., 'Greater Paris and its lessons for metropolitan strategic planning', *Town Planning Review* (2018), 89(1).

Duyvendak, J.W. *The Power of Politics. New Social Movements in France* (Boulder, Colorado: Westview Press, 1995)

Gardesse, C., 'The fraught 'menage à trois' of public actors, private players and inhabitants: Problems of participation in French urban development projects', *Urban Studies* (2015) vol. 52(16).

Gilli, F., 'Sprawl or reagglomeration? The dynamics of employment deconcentration and industrial transformation in Greater Paris', *Urban Studies* (2009), vol. 46, issue 7

Halbert, L., 'The polycentric city region that never was: The Paris agglomeration, Bassin Parisien and spatial planning strategies in France', *Built Environment* (2006) 32(2).

Harvey, D., *Paris Capital of Modernity* (New York, London: Routledge, 2003)

Heathcott, J., 'The Promenade Plantée: Politics, Planning, and Urban Design in Postindustrial Paris'. *Journal of Planning Education and Research* (2013) 33(3).

Nez, H., 'De l'expertise associative à la constitution d'un contre-pouvoir. Action collective et concertation à Paris Rive Gauche', *Espaces et Sociétés* (2012) 3(1),

Préteceille, E., 'Has ethno-racial segregation increased in the greater Paris metropolitan area?' *Revue Francaise de Sociologie* (2011) vol. 52,

Rabbiosi, C., 'Renewing a historical legacy: Tourism, leisure shopping and urban branding in Paris', *Cities* (2015) vol. 42, Part B

Rougé, N. and Vilie, U. A., 'Clichy-Batignolles: Where urban planning meets the climate', *OECD Observer* (2015) 304

Sintomer, Y., 'Participatory Democracy and Governance: Local Politics in France', ECPR 29th Sessions of Workshops (2001), Université Grenoble

Tardieu, C., 'Transition énergétique dans les projets urbains: conditions de mise en œuvre. Analyse des cas Paris Rive Gauche, Clichy-Batignolles et Paris Nord Est', doctoral dissertation (2015), Université Lille1

Vivant, E., 'How Underground Culture is Changing Paris', *Urban Research & Practice* (2009) vol. 2

Waterhout, B., Othengrafen, F., & Sykes, O. (2013). Neo-liberalization Processes and Spatial Planning in France, Germany, and the Netherlands: An Exploration. *Planning Practice and Research, 28*(1), 141–159.

Widmer, C., and Kubler, D., 'Regenerating urban neighbourhoods in Europe. Eight case Studies in six European Countries', *ZDA Working Paper* (2014) issue 3

LYON

Engaging in Civic Dialogues

Citizen Involvement in the Lyon Metropolis

Lilian van Karnenbeek and Roelof Verhage

Since the turn of the century, like many other cities in Western Europe, citizen involvement has become increasingly advocated in the Lyon Metropolis. The Metropolis currently has grand ambitions for citizen involvement: from its own website, it aims to '*Développer une démocratie plus décentralisée et plus participative, tel est l'objectif que s'est assigné le Grand Lyon*.'[1] Translated as setting an objective to develop a more decentralized and participatory urban democracy, the public authority stresses the importance of dialogue with citizens. With this aim, the Lyon Metropolis builds on the ambitious and ground-breaking *Charte de la participation*, developed in 2003 by the *Communauté Urbaine de Lyon* (since replaced by the administrative entity of *Métropole Lyon*, or Lyon Metropolis). With the *Charte*, Lyon was the first intermunicipal body of France to formulate a general participation policy. At the same time, and just like the rest of France, the political landscape of the Lyon Metropolis is strongly shaped by principles of representative democracy. Although residents' direct participation in planning decisions is therefore limited, their voice is heard through elected representatives and an evolving process of concertation. This framework of representative democracy underpins the approach of Lyon Metropolis to citizen involvement in the field of planning. Alongside is a palpable legacy of economic growth, industry and prosperity in Lyon, all of which have helped

1 Translation: 'Developing a more decentralized and participatory democracy is the objective of Greater Lyon.' Grand Lyon, 'Les instances de concertation – La Métropole de Lyon', 2021a). Online. Available HTTP: grandlyon.com/metropole/instances-concertation.html

shape a defining intrinsic logic of the city: a neoliberal energy and spirit of independence.

The Lyon Metropolis

Comprising the city of Lyon and surrounding suburban communes, the Lyon Metropolis is France's second-largest metropolis, situated in the Auvergne-Rhône-Alpes region of south-east France. The Lyon Metropolis has 1.3 million inhabitants and includes 59 municipalities, of which that of Lyon is the largest and the most central.[2] The Metropolis is surrounded by hills and is located at the confluence of the rivers Saône and Rhône. Historically, this strategic location at the crossroads between Northern Europe and the Mediterranean Sea, close to Italy and the Alps, has made Lyon an attractive location for commerce and manufacturing. In particular, Lyon became an important centre for textiles production during the Renaissance. In 1536, its burgeoning silk industry expanded under King François I, who granted Lyon a monopoly on importing raw silk in to France. During the Industrial Revolution, an established and varied textile industry led to a substantial rise in mechanical and chemical manufacturing, with both industries still dominating Lyon's industrial landscape today. This centuries-long legacy of production and trade has guaranteed Lyon a thriving economy which in turn has created conditions for a formative characteristic of the metropolis: a neoliberal, independent spirit. With an emphasis on economic growth, this spirit has been a leading principle for the governance of Lyon during the 2000s. It should be noted that currently, Lyon is at a crossroads: during the 2020 elections, the political party *Europe Écologie-Les Verts*, in an alliance with left-wing parties, obtained a majority both at the level of the municipality of Lyon, and at the level of the Metropolis. Their win put an end to almost two decades of reign by Gérard Collomb, who combined the positions of Mayor of Lyon with the presidency of the Metropolis to roll out his neoliberal-inspired policy of urban development. The extent of change to urban policies this will induce is not yet clear, but a move away from the neoliberal policy model seems probable.

The footprints of Lyon's economic growth are also visible in its spatial patterns. In the nineteenth century, for example, silk making was concentrated in

2 Agence d'Urbanisme, *Lexique métropolitain: les territoires lyonnais* (Lyon: Agence d'urbanisme, 2018)

Croix-Rousse, a hilly neighbourhood situated at the left bank of the Saône. The area is notable for its narrow, winding streets and covered passageways, or *traboules,* that were once used to securely transport silk. When modern industries came to Lyon in the nineteenth century, rapid population growth put tremendous pressure on the city centre. Correspondingly, the city expanded its urban developments to the right banks of the Rhône. As its economic strength grew, Lyon continued to spread widely by annexing surrounding (rural) land and villages into the first half of the twentieth century. Decades later, another population increase in the aftermath of the Second World War compelled the city to expand further eastwards. But while Lyon annexed surrounding areas, signs of social polarization crystallized. The economic wealth benefitted a limited group, who segregated themselves from the poor and settled in affluent neighbourhoods. Those neighbourhoods are situated in the western part of the metropolis, while the poorer areas are concentrated in the east, in large-scale and high-rise social housing areas. The upturn in Lyon's economy thus also had negative consequences over the years. In a ripple effect, spatial inequalities occurred.

A Representative Democracy

As across all of France, the Lyon Metropolis is led by principles of representative democracy. Based on citizens equally and directly electing representatives – that is, persons who may legitimately act on behalf of the public – representative democracy is intrinsically linked to republican logic. In other words, the government is supposed to be the representative of the public interest. The idea of representative democracy gained momentum in France in 1789, the year the French Revolution began. In the decade that followed, the political landscape of the country was radically changed. The preceding Ancient Regime – a privileged corporatist system founded by feudalists and monarchs – was abolished and the First French Republic was officially proclaimed in September 1792. Even more importantly, the prevailing republican logic elevated the interests of the public above those of intermediary bodies such as privileged guilds and parishes. Fast-forward to today, France continues to embrace representative democracy. The model remains in conflict with corporate groups which by definition represent the interests of specific communities. Obviously, and in practice, this coexistence is more complex and nuanced than a simple banning of corporatism in favour of increased focus on public interests, yet this dogma enormously shaped (and still shapes) the political landscape in France.

Representative Democracy and Urban Planning

The principles of representative democracy not only highly determined the political landscape of France, but also its urban planning. Following this representative tradition, the government has the strongest say in urban planning. We take a jump in time here and go to the years right after the Second World War, when urban planning developed strongly in France. In the aftermath of the conflict, France was a highly centralized country. The centralist approach applied to the field of urban planning, in which the State invoked its instrumental rationality and comprehensive knowledge to position itself 'above' others, resulting in centralized laws and detailed plans. However, from the 1960s on, the State slowly began to lose its belief in full centralism and started to move towards the principle of decentralization. Scattered throughout France, it created intermunicipal bodies to better advance the control of social and environmental challenges, and strengthen economic development. Known as *Communautés Urbaine,* the first four of these intermunicipal bodies were created by the State in 1969; among them was the *Communauté Urbaine de Grand Lyon.* But although decentralization was set in motion, urban planning remained a strongly centralized state affair.

The decentralization laws established by former Minister of the Interior, Gaston Defferre between 1982 and 1983 profoundly changed this. With these laws, numerous powers and responsibilities of the State, including powers and responsibilities in urban planning, were devolved to the municipalities. In the case of Lyon, they were transferred to the intermunicipal level, due to the existence of the *Communauté Urbaine de Grand Lyon.* As a result, the planning authority at the state level disappeared and local planning authorities were created at different levels and for different areas. In keeping with the tradition of representative democracy, their remit is to work for public benefit at a local level – all the while keeping in line with national interests. But despite taking a significant step towards decentralization, the State nevertheless retains control: only the State can determine the application, directives and objectives of French planning law, or *Code de l'urbanisme.* Nevertheless, the legislation affords a great deal of liberty to local planning authorities. In 2015, the *Communautés Urbaine* were replaced by the administrative entity Metropolis, gaining greater jurisdiction by the MAPTAM law (*Modernisation de l'Action Publique Territorial et d'Affirmation des Métropoles*) of 2014.

The Representation of Citizens in Urban Planning

From presidents to municipal councillors, France's representative democracy sees citizens directly elect their representatives from national to local. Since the creation of Metropolises as an administrative entity, yet another layer of governance has come into existence: metropolitan councils. Although usually comprising a delegation of the municipal council, Lyon is unique in being the only Metropolis with a directly elected metropolitan council since 2020.[3] In the Lyon Metropolis citizens are in a strong position as they vote for their municipal and metropolitan councils. In keeping with traditions of representative democracy, council members must represent the interests of the citizenry. As most urban planning decisions are undertaken by the Metropolis, the metropolitan council is therefore responsible for representing the public interest in urban planning.

Despite these representative principles, urban planning moves beyond mere representation by elected persons. In planning laws, such as the *Code de l'urbanisme*, the French legislator frequently uses the word *concertation*. Literally, the term refers to dialogues with citizens and private actors such as developers and landowners. But its legal definition stretches no further than the public authority's duty to organize public hearings and to publish information about urban development projects. Consequently, citizen involvement in France tends to remain at the lowest rungs of the ladder of Arnstein:[4] it hardly goes beyond consultation. The republican logic does not allow admitting the legitimacy of individuals, community organizations or lobby groups in intervening in public decisions. It is within this context that citizen involvement rarely results in direct participation, or arrangements such as co-production and co-development. Nevertheless, the issue of citizen participation is gaining importance in France lately, in particular in the field of urban planning.[5] The Lyon Metropolis is no exception to this statement.

---

3 Grand Lyon, 'Élections métropolitaines 2020,' Online. Available HTTP: https://www.grandlyon.com/metropole/elections-metropolitaines-2020.html

4 S. Arnstein,'A Ladder of Citizen Participation', *Journal of the American Institute of Planners* (1969), 35 (4), 216-224

5 C. Gardesse, 'The fraught 'menage à trois' of public actors, private players and inhabitants: Problems of participation in French urban development projects', *Urban Studies* (2015) 52 (16), 3035–3053

Governance Structures in and Around the Lyon Metropolis

In 2015, the Lyon Metropolis became an independent administrative entity at the metropolitan level in France. The Metropolis is chaired by a president and controlled by a directly elected metropolitan council. The metropolitan council was dominated by moderates at first, who had a liberal approach to urban policies. However, in the 2020 elections, the Green party (*Europe Écologie-Les Verts*) in an alliance with left-wing parties obtained a majority in the metropolitan council.[6] Operating above and beyond the remit of the 59 municipalities that make up the Lyon Metropolis, the strategic spatial plan, *Schéma de Cohérence Territoriale* is overseen by an intermunicipal body that manages planning decisions in an area slightly larger than the Metropolis' borders. It includes the airport *Saint-Exupery* and its surrounding business districts. Further expanding, the Lyon Metropolis collaborates in the *Pôle Métropolitain*, including towns of Saint-Etienne Vienne, Bourgoin-Jallieu and Villefranche. The *Pôle Métropolitain* has been created as an informal cooperation structure in reaction to the extended influence of the Lyon Metropolis beyond its boundaries. The *Pôle Métropolitain* particularly focuses its attention on topics such as economy and mobility.[7]

Urban Planning in the Lyon Metropolis

Since the decentralization laws, urban planning has been an intermunicipal affair. Today, the Lyon Metropolis has the most powers in urban planning and related fields, such as public transport, economic development, culture, housing and environmental matters. During the last decades, Lyon Metropolis has used these powers in the development of several large-scale urban projects. Lyon Confluence, Part-Dieu and Carré de Soie are current, determinant development projects to plan and design the Metropolis. The urban project Lyon Confluence, which comprises housing, offices, commerce, and public space, redevelops the former industrial and harbour area of the city centre. The urban project transforms an industrial wasteland into a sustainable extension of the nearby city centre, while

---

6 A. Mestre and S. Zappi, *Le Monde*, 'Les leçons des municipales pour la gauche : alliances victorieuses PS-EELV, érosion du PCF, LFI invisible', 30 June 2020. Online. Available HTTP: https://www.lemonde.fr/politique/article/2020/06/30/le-ps-et-eelv-forment-un-nouveau-duo-gagnant-a-gauche_6044640_823448.html

7 Agence d'Urbanisme, *Lexique métropolitain: les territoires lyonnais* (Lyon: Agence d'urbanisme, 2018)

retaining some of the unique industrial and harbour architecture. Lyon's central business district surrounding the central railway station, Part-Dieu, is also being developed into an attractive area offering potentials for Lyon's tertiary district to grow. The urban project Carré de Soie aims to reduce spatial inequality by redeveloping a former mixed residential and industrial area, initially developed largely in connection with an important artificial silk manufacturing plant in the eastern part of the Lyon Metropolis. The project comprises housing, offices and public facilities and aims to contribute to the revitalization of the eastern part of the Metropolis that suffers from high unemployment rates and poor housing conditions. The influence of the Lyon Metropolis differs between these projects. In Lyon Confluence, for example, the Metropolis was directly involved in the development project as landowner and developer. In the Carré de Soie and Part Dieu projects, the land ownership was predominantly private, and the role of the Metropolis was limited to the facilitation and regulation of private initiatives. Despite the role of the Lyon Metropolis in these and other projects, the municipalities also have a certain influence: the municipalities sign building permits and are in charge of the realization and maintenance of public spaces and facilities.

Citizen Involvement in the Lyon Metropolis

Despite being written 15 years ago, the general participation policy of the *Communauté Urbaine de Lyon* was remarkably forward-thinking in its description of the multiple layers of citizen involvement. In the policy five different levels are distinguished, ranging from informing to co-developing.[8] These levels determine the relationships between the intermunicipal (now: metropolitan) government and citizens. The first, 'informing', relates to the government letting citizens know about intentions, decisions and actions. At the second level, 'bottom-up information', the government (or citizens) organizes activities to uncover civic expectations, for example through surveys, notebooks and petitions. The third is 'consultation': the government asking the opinions of citizens on a particular project or decision. Public inquiries and local referenda are examples of consultation instruments. The fourth level is called 'concertation' and refers to a dialogue between citizens and the government on a particular subject. Organized by the government, it aims to further explore the opinions of citizens while bringing public interest to the fore. The last type of involvement is 'co-development'. At this level, the government invites citizens or other actors to participate in a development project or to maintain a particular area.

---

8 Grand Lyon, 'Charte de la participation du Grand Lyon', (Lyon: Grand Lyon, 2003)

The Lyon Metropolis gives most priority to concertation, which corresponds with the French planning law. It is believed that concertation enhances legitimacy, clarity and transparency of government actions; promotes dissemination; ensures understanding of the public interest; increases the diversity and exchange of opinions. Furthermore, concertation procedures aim to advance efficiency by improving public service delivery and adapting projects and decisions to meet citizens' expectations. In addition to concertation procedures, the Lyon Metropolis set up an advisory board in May 2015, known as *Conseil de Développement*.[9] The advisory board does not question the findings and direction of the elected representatives, but gives information to representatives or helps with concertation procedures. The advisory board consist of a variety of actors, ranging from voluntary citizens and citizens groups, to local entrepreneurs and cultural groups. They give voice to local people, and strengthen the exchange between organized and unorganized groups through dialogues and reflections. The elected representatives can ask the board for advice or receive unsolicited advice. To illustrate how citizen involvement takes place in practice in Lyon Metropolis, the urban project Carré de Soie serves as a useful case study.

Citizen involvement in the Carré de Soie urban development

The urban project

Carré de Soie is situated in the eastern part of the Lyon Metropolis, in the municipalities of Vaulx-en-Velin and Villeurbanne. The neighbourhood has a long history in the textile industries, the production of artificial silk (viscose) in particular. In the aftermath of the Second World War, and exaggerated by the economic crisis of the 1970s, a decline in industrial activities spelled the end for textile manufacturing in Lyon. An outcome of the steep downturn in industries was abandoned houses and factories. For decades, Carré de Soie has not attracted any (public) investment, resulting in degradation of the urban quality of the area, and generally contributing to a poor reputation. At the turn of the twenty-first century, however, the situation began to alter. Around this time, various organizations

9 Grand Lyon, Le Conseil de développement de la Métropole de Lyon, 2021e. Online. Available HTTP: https://www.grandlyon.com/metropole/le-conseil-de-developpement.html

showed an interest in Carré de Soie: cinema chain Gaumont Pathé build a cinema complex; the Rhône administrative *département* reopened a railway line between the city centre and the airport. These investments in the area prompted the mayor of Vaulx-en-Velin to request the Lyon Metropolis to make further investments. The Lyon Metropolis responded to the request and seized the opportunity to launch the urban development project, Carré de Soie, alongside investments in a leisure centre, metro and bus lines.

Consequently, Carré de Soie was to develop towards a high-density, sustainable and mixed-use neighbourhood. Started in 2004 and projected for completion by 2030, the development was based on an incremental development strategy,[10] that implied a stepwise development pathway from one location to the next. Throughout the 500 hectares site, private developers were allowed to buy specific plots of land, with the Lyon Metropolis acquiring strategic parcels. Moreover, the urban project was guided by a spatial concept which prioritized green space provision. This provision was deemed particularly important due to the infertile and polluted ground caused by previous industrial activities. To that end, the concept included a canopy of trees, a green promenade that stretched from north to south, and the development of garden islands. The Lyon Metropolis established Mission Carré de Soie, a delegation of the Metropolis, to officially coordinate the project.

The First Level: Informing

The involved public authorities took various measures to inform citizens about the urban development project. The Lyon Metropolis and the municipalities of Vaulx-en-Velin and Villeurbanne opened a so-called *Maison du Projet*: an information centre that is accessible to everyone during weekdays. The *Maison du Projet* features documents, exhibitions and interactive models about the development. Furthermore, the information centre is the workplace for civil servants working on the Carré de Soie development. In addition to the *Maison du Projet*, citizens can get information by subscribing to a newsletter and visiting the website of the urban development, which features development locations, policy documents, concertation and current affairs.

---

10 L. Van Karnenbeek, *Creating the city step-by-step. When incremental development strategies meet institutions*, (Wageningen: Wageningen University & Research, 2020)

The Fourth Level: Concertation

In following the commitments outlined in its 2003 participation policy, Lyon Metropolis prioritized concertation in de Carré de Soie development, with multiple rounds organized. At the beginning of the project, public gatherings were called to communicate initial steps of the overall development. During these gatherings, the involved authorities informed the citizens, who in turn were given opportunities for dialogue. After these gatherings, concertation was organized per development location. The process employed a range of communication tools, including presentations, debates based on sketches of maps and photos, site visits, workshops, discussion rounds, and lists of recommendations. Most of these concertation procedures centred on public spaces. At one of the development locations, a former artificial silk production plant called TASE Factory, the design of a green space – Esplanade TASE – saw citizens work with urban planners and architects. Organized by Lyon Metropolis, the collaboration resembled co-development, the fifth level of citizen involvement in the 2003 participation policy. This co-development was considered highly innovative, particularly compared to the usual concertation procedures.

The concertation of inhabitants is further facilitated by the *Conseils de quartier*, or neighbourhood councils. With the law on local democracy of 2002 – known as the *loi relative à la démocratie de proximité* – the creation of these councils is obligatory in municipalities of more than 80,000 inhabitants. Because the area of Carré de Soie concerns two municipalities, there are two *Conseils de quartier*. These councils are created on the initiative of the municipalities to promote direct exchanges between citizens and elected officials. They have a board composed of elected officials, and representatives of inhabitants, associations, private companies and public organizations. They regularly organize meetings that are open to everyone. During these meetings, they address all kinds of issues, ranging from housing and urban planning to health, education and culture. Mission Carré de Soie provides technical support, and the ideas and observations of the councils are officially presented to the mayor (or vice mayor) in regular meetings. These meetings are planned at least three times a year but can be more frequent if there are topical issues to address. The councils are important actors in the concertation process in the Carré de Soie development.

Citizen Activism

Citizen involvement in Carré de Soie is mainly based on information and concertation. Nevertheless, the influence of citizens may also move beyond these formal arrangements, as the development location TASE shows. The land of the

17-hectare site of a former silk factory was bought by a private developer who proposed a development plan for a 75,000 sqm project with high-rise residential towers. Within the plan of the developer, the historic factory had to be demolished. In reaction to the development plan, the citizens of Vaulx-en-Velin mobilized, organizing themselves in an association to protect the historical building which they considered important industrial heritage. To protect the building, they legally challenged the building permits for two of the residential towers. As a result of this legal challenge, the entire TASE development had to stop: the development could only continue once citizens withdrew their legal challenges. The protest forced the private developer, the Lyon Metropolis and the Municipality of Vaulx-en-Velin to negotiate a renewed development plan. After almost two years, an agreement was reached. In this renewed plan, the private developer preserved the main factory building and renovated it with respect to the existing architecture. This example shows the powers of mobilized groups of citizens, beyond the official levels of involvement such as informing and concertation.

Discussion

In the Carré de Soie development, citizen involvement is mostly organized through concertation. As a consequence, the involvement of citizens is generally reactive. Citizens are asked to express their opinions about the projects or development plans that are communicated by the planning authority. The creation of the *Conseils de quartier*, with an agenda-setting capacity, does change the influence of citizens slightly: they have the ability to set topics on the public agenda. But their degree of liberty depends strongly on the will of the concerned planning authorities. In some instances, the planning authorities are even criticized for leaning too heavily on citizens. It raises questions about how the wider process relates to the representation of citizens. The bottom-up mobilization against the demolition of the TASE factory illustrates that there are also possibilities for citizens to intervene in the definition of urban development projects. However, the influence of citizens goes through opposition and conflict rather than through involvement or participation. Generally speaking, citizens in the Carré de Soie development mainly rely on the vastly institutionalized form of concertation. In current conditions, it does not appear that partnerships between public actors and citizens proceed to a model of participation on an equal basis.

Conclusion

For all of its neoliberal character and spirit of independence, the Lyon Metropolis nevertheless falls in line with the rest of France when it comes to citizen involvement. That is to say, it can only be understood in the context of the broader French political landscape. The legacy of the French Revolution clearly positioned citizens at the heart of representative democracy: they are represented by elected officials. Hence, the republican logic and representative tradition highly determine the relationship between the government and citizens in urban planning. Although citizens (and other interest groups) have little direct access to decision making in urban planning, they are represented by elected representatives. France's decentralization and metropolitan laws had a profound impact on urban planning: most notably, representation at the local and metropolitan level gained importance. The path towards decentralization showed that the French State is not impermeable to initiatives towards local representation. Representation in urban planning is therefore particularly shaped by the values of local politics. The municipal and metropolitan council currently represent citizens in the Lyon Metropolis, illustrating how representation at the local level is still highly valued. The Lyon Metropolis is particularly praised for being the first in France with a directly elected metropolitan council.

Despite the importance of representation, citizens are involved in urban planning matters through concertation, a legally prescribed procedure. It is the public authority's duty to organize public hearings and publish information about urban development projects. The Lyon Metropolis has developed a broader meaning of concertation: it refers to dialogues with citizens. Since the turn of the twenty-first century, the Lyon Metropolis has increasingly prioritized citizen involvement. Its government was the first to formulate a general participation policy, in which they placed particular emphasis on concertation. Over the years, the position of citizens in concertation has been strengthened by various factors, including the establishment of the metropolitan and neighbourhood councils. The Carré de Soie development exemplifies a strengthened concertation procedure. Despite the strong notion of representation and concertation, the Lyon Metropolis is exploring the meaning of participation. The cooperation of citizens, planners and architects in the TASE development location is an example of such a participative initiative. Nevertheless, the Lyon Metropolis holds the strongest position, with representation and concertation as core principles. The adherence to the republican model in a representative democracy still suppresses more extensive types of citizen involvement, such as direct citizen participation.

Bibliography

Agence d'Urbanisme, *Lexique métropolitain: les territoires lyonnais* (Lyon: Agence d'urbanisme, 2018)

Arnstein, S., 'A Ladder of Citizen Participation', *Journal of the American Institute of Planners* (1969), 35 (4), 216-224

Booth, P., 'Planning and the Culture of Governance: Local Institutions and Reform in France', *European Planning Studies* (2009) 17(5), 677-695

Bourdin, S. and Torre A., 'The territorial big bang: which assessment about the territorial reform in France?' *European Planning Studies* (2020)

Carpenter, J. and Verhage R., 'Lyon City Profile', *Cities* (2014) 38, 57-68

De Oliveira, P., 'Imagining an Old City in Nineteenth-Century France: Urban Renovation, Civil Society, and the Making of Vieux Lyon'. *Journal of Urban History* (2019) 45 (1), 67-98

Foret, C., 'De l'épopée industrielle de l'Est lyonnais au projet urbain du Carré de Soie, ou l'invention d'un territoire d'agglomeration (Lyon: Agence d'Urbanisme, 2010)

Gardesse, C., 'The fraught 'menage à trois' of public actors, private players and inhabitants: Problems of participation in French urban development projects', *Urban Studies* (2015) 52 (16), 3035–3053

Gardesse, C. and Zetlaoui-Léger, J., 'Citizen participation: an essential lever for urban transformation in France?', in: Brownill, S. and Bradley, Q. (eds.), *Localism and Neighbourhood Planning: Power to the People?* (Bristol: Policy Press, 2017), 199-214

Grand Lyon, 'Charte de la participation du Grand Lyon', (Lyon: Grand Lyon, 2003)

Grand Lyon, 'Accessible, vivant, ouvert, Carré de Soie se réinvente', 2018. Online. Available HTTP: https://carredesoie.grandlyon.com/

Grand Lyon, 'Élections métropolitaines 2020', Online. Available HTTP: https://www.grandlyon.com/metropole/elections-metropolitaines-2020.html

Grand Lyon, 'Les instances de concertation - La Métropole de Lyon', 2021a. Online. Available HTTP: https://www.grandlyon.com/metropole/instances-concertation.html

Grand Lyon, 'Lyon Confluence', 2021b. Online. Available HTTP: https://www.grandlyon.com/actions/lyon-confluence.html

Grand Lyon, 'Lyon Part Dieu', 2021c. Online. Available HTTP : https://www.grandlyon.com/actions/lyon-part-dieu.html

Grand Lyon, 'Carré de Soie', 2021d. Online. Available HTTP: https://www.grandlyon.com/actions/vaulx-en-velin-villeurbanne-carre-de-soie.html

Grand Lyon, 'Le Conseil de développement de la Métropole de Lyon', 2021e. Online. Available HTTP: https://www.grandlyon.com/metropole/le-conseil-de-developpement.html

Grand Lyon, 'Concertation', 2021f . Online. Available HTTP: https://carredesoie.grandlyon.com/projet/concertation/

Grand Lyon, 'La concertation sur le projet Carré de Soie', 2021g. Online. Available HTTP: https://www.grandlyon.com/actions/concertation-carre-de-soie.html

Guironnet, A., 'Une financiarisation si discrete ? La circulation des standards de la filière d'investissement en immobilier tertiaire dans les politiques de développpment urbain du Grand Lyon', *Métropoles* (2016) 19

Janvier, Y., 'Nouveaux enjeux de société', in: Martinand, C., and Landrieu, J., *L'aménagement en questions* (Paris: Association des Etudes Foncières, 1996)

Karadimitrio, N., Magalhaes, C. de., and Verhage R., *Planning, Risk and Property Development. Urban regeneration in England, France and the Netherlands* (New York: Routledge, 2013)

Mestre, A., and Zappi, S., *Le Monde*, 'Les leçons des municipales pour la gauche : alliances victorieuses PS-EELV, érosion du PCF, LFI invisible', 30 June 2020. Online. Available HTTP: https://www.lemonde.fr/politique/article/2020/06/30/le-ps-et-eelv-forment-un-nouveau-duo-gagnant-a-gauche_6044640_823448.html

Manin, B., *Le gouvernement représentatif* (Paris: Calmann-Levy, 1995)

Rosanvallon, P., *L'Etat en France de 1789 à nos jours. Collection points histoire* (Paris: Editions du Seuil, 1990)

Rosales-Montano, S., Aguiléra, A., Mignot, D., and Terral, L., *L'expérience métropolitaine Lyonnaise* (Paris: Editions Gallimard, 2015)

Saurugger, S., 'Representative versus participatory democracy? France, Europe and civil society,' *Paper presented at the 2020 ECPR Joint Sessions of Workshops*, University of Uppsala, Sweden.

Thoenig, J., *L'ère des technocrats* (Paris: L'Harmattan, 1987)

Van Karnenbeek, L., 'Greening the city between public needs and private preferences in Carré de Soie, Lyon', *Town Planning Review* (forthcoming)

Van Karnenbeek, L., *Creating the city step-by-step. When incremental development strategies meet institutions.* (Wageningen: Wageningen University & Research, 2020)

About the authors

Foreword

Martina Löw is professor of sociology at the Technische Universität Berlin, Germany. Her areas of specialization and research are sociological theory, urban sociology, space theory and cultural sociology. She was visiting professor and held fellowships at universities in Gothenburg (Sweden), Salvador da Bahia (Brazil), St. Gallen (Switzerland), Paris (France) and Vienna (Austria). From 2011 until 2013 she was president of the German Sociological Association. Currently she is head of the Collaborative Research Centre "Re-Figuration of Spaces" (DFG).

Introduction and Paris

Menno van der Veen aims to smile more often. He is a researcher and practitioner at Tertium. He received his master's degrees in law and philosophy at the University of Amsterdam. His PhD research (TU Delt) was about relational contracts in urban development projects. In his current research he focuses on contractual perspectives of citizen participation in urban development.

Jan Willem Duyvendak is Distinguished Research Professor of Sociology at the University of Amsterdam. His main fields of research currently are the transformation of the welfare state, belonging and 'feeling at home,' and nativism. He is currently rector of the Netherlands Institute for Advanced Study in the Humanities and Social Sciences at the Royal Netherlands Academy of Arts and Sciences (NIAS-KNAW).

Berlin and Amsterdam

Karin Christof is an architect and researcher, affiliated as a PhD candidate with the University of Amsterdam. Through ethnographically inspired fieldwork, her research explores the values that citizen initiatives uphold when re-purposing derelict buildings for the common good. Her fields of interest are urban governance, people's right to the city, economic independence and social equality.

Franziska Sack is an architect. Her practice spans both design and construction as well as practice-based research. She worked as a teaching and research assistant at the TU Berlin with a focus on participatory design-build projects. Recently, her work field has expanded to spatial aspects of sustainable mobility at Smart City | DB.

Stan Majoor is an urban planner and political scientist and employed as professor of coordination of urban issues and director of the Centre of Expertise Urban Governance and Social Innovation at the Amsterdam University of Applied Sciences. His fields of interest are urban governance, spatial planning, public participation and practice-oriented research.

Groningen

Melika Levelt is senior researcher at the Centre of Expertise Urban Technology, Amsterdam University of Applied Sciences. Trained as an economic geographer her research interests have broadened towards planning and governance for sustainable cities with projects on food, logistics, urban green and energy. Melika is editor-in-chief of the Dutch-Flemish spatial planning journal, *Rooilijn*.

Wendy Tan is senior researcher at Wageningen University and Research. Her research expertise focuses on the implementation of land use and transportation integration, mobility issues and institutional perspective in planning processes in Europe, America and Southeast Asia.

Peter Bootsma is the first appointed 'Green Mayor' for the city of Groningen. As a voluntary ambassador and ombudsman for climate adaptation, Peter is fighting for more green and less hardened surfaces in the city. Peter is also chairperson of Noorden Duurzaam, a regional network association in the North of the Netherlands of public and private stakeholders actively contributing to speeding up the sustainability transition. Peter shares his expertise in organization management and management studies to innovate for sustainable and democratic processes in society.

Mustafa Hasanov is a postdoctoral researcher at Wageningen University & Research. His PhD research focused on the role of community self-organisation and local collective action in the context of sustainability transformations in Groningen. Currently, his research is exploring aspects of cultural innovation in managing sustainability transitions and the role of community-based organisations in the delivery of sustainable, resilient, and socially just developments in food systems. He is the book review officer of the Royal Geographical Society (with IBG) Food Geographies Working Group.

Hamburg

Renée Tribble is trained as an architect and is an independent urban planner. Currently she holds a visiting professorship for urban development planning and management at the University of Kassel. She is a founding member and partner of PlanBude Hamburg. She focuses on the conception, advice and organization of urban development processes, participatory and cooperative planning, urban practice, art and alternative urban development.

Cathrin Zengerling is a legal scholar and works primarily in the areas of (international) environmental, energy and planning law, as well as sustainable urban development. She heads the junior professorship 'Transformation to Sustainable Energy Systems' and the research group 'Urban Footprints' at the University of Freiburg.

Michiel Stapper has a background in geography, philosophy and sociology. He recently defended his PhD dissertation, 'Do contracts have politics?' His research interests lie at the intersection of cities, society and law. Currently he is employed as an assistant professor at Tilburg Law School and is part of the public law and governance department.

Lyon

Lilian van Karnenbeek is a postdoctoral researcher at the Institute of Jurisprudence, Constitutional and Administrative Law, Utrecht University. Lilian conducts research on planning law, institutions and urban development. She holds a PhD in urban planning from Wageningen University and Research, a master's degree in urban planning from the University of Amsterdam, and a bachelor's degree in human geography and spatial planning from Utrecht University.

Roelof Verhage is a lecturer in urban planning, and director of the Institut d'Urbanisme de Lyon at Université Lyon 2. His research interests are in urban development and urban regeneration, with a particular attention on land policy and the operation of the planning system. Much of his work has a cross-national comparative character, concentrating on countries in Western Europe.

Copy Editor

Frances Arnold is a British writer, editor and journalist. With a particular focus on art, design, cultural ecosystems and cities, she has written for international publications including *Art Asia Pacific*, *Artsy*, *The Economist*, *Frame* and others. She is also a content provider for architecture studios, sustainability platforms, and social enterprises.

Acknowledgements

The authors would like to thank the following people for sharing their time, experiences and perspectives:

Jochum Admiraal, Julien Antelin, Martin Assink, Clement Boisseuil, Dickel Bokoum, Daniela Brahm, Frank Brander, Marco Cremaschi, David Crommentuijn, Agnès Deboulet, Peter Dortwegt, Jaap Draaisma, Jesko Fezer, Tom Frantzen, Patrick Le Galès, Ed García Conde, Frederic Gili, Eva Gladek, Harko van den Hende, Andrea Hofmann, Jurgen Hoogendorn, Hendrik Hübscher, Greg Lloyd, Martina Löw, John Mollenkopf, Luigi Mustafov, Wilko Eskes, Koen Esselink, Marja ter Horst, Frans Kerver, Jos Meijers, Christina Pachaly, Deborah Peel, Antina van der Ploeg, Annemiek Rijckenberg, Willem Salet, Roeland van der Schaaf, Samuli Schielke, Kim von Schönfeld, Laurens Stiekema, Gerard Tolner, Jorne Visser, Tommaso Vitale, Hiltje van der Wal, Janin Walter, and Carina Wiekens.